TOGETH>R

Presents:

PLAY IT FORWARD

TOGETHXR

Presents:

PLAY IT FORWARD

HOW WOMEN ARE CHANGING SPORTS TO CHANGE THE WORLD

Edited by Leila Sales
Foreword by Alex Morgan
Afterword by Sue Bird
Artwork by Mel Cerri

CHRONICLE BOOKS
SAN FRANCISCO

Library of Congress Cataloging-in-Publication Data
Names: Sales, Leila, editor. | Morgan, Alex (Alexandra Patricia), 1989-
author of foreword. | Bird, Sue, 1980- author of afterword. | Cerri, Mel, artist.
Title: Play it forward : how women are changing sports to change the world /
edited by Leila Sales ; foreword by Alex Morgan ; afterword by Sue Bird; artwork by Mel Cerri.
Description: San Francisco : Chronicle Books, [2025] |
At head of title: TOGETHXR presents.
Identifiers: LCCN 2024029626 | ISBN 9781797232171 (hardcover)
Subjects: LCSH: Women athletes--Biography. | Women Olympic
athletes--Biography. | Women athletes--History. | Women Olympic
athletes--History. | Sex discrimination in sports. | Sex discrimination
against women. | Courage. | Leadership in women. | Resilience
(Personality trait) | Women social reformers--Biography.
Classification: LCC GV697.A1 P5535 2025 | DDC 796.092/52--dc23/eng/20240812
LC record available at https://lccn.loc.gov/2024029626

Manufactured in China.

MIX
Paper | Supporting
responsible forestry
FSC™ C008047
FSC
www.fsc.org

Design by Maggie Edelman.

Artwork by Mel Cerri.

Front cover photographs © Associated Press.
Angel McCoughtry (top left) photo by AnthonyNesmith/
Cal Sport Media (Cal Sport Media via AP Images); Daria Kasatkina (bottom left)
AP Photo/Petr David Josek; Solai Washington (bottom right) photo by
Patricia Pérez Ferraro/SPP/Sipa USA (Sipa via AP Images).

Back cover photograph © TOGETHXR.

See page 224 for interior photo credits.

10 9 8 7 6 5 4 3 2 1

Chronicle books and gifts are available at special quantity discounts to
corporations, professional associations, literacy programs, and other organizations.
For details and discount information, please contact our premiums department
at corporategifts@chroniclebooks.com or at 1-800-759-0190.

Chronicle Books LLC
680 Second Street
San Francisco, California 94107
www.chroniclebooks.com

DEDICATED TO THE CULTURE SHAPERS, BARRIER BREAKERS, AND GLASS SHATTERERS FROM THEN TO NOW, AND TO COME.

CONTENTS

FOREWORD

For too long, female athletes have been kept in the margins. Women's sports have been undervalued and underinvested. I've experienced this firsthand. My teammates have experienced this firsthand. The barrier breakers you'll read about in this book have experienced this firsthand. But, in my opinion, changing this all starts with a story. The more visible we are—the more stories we tell, the more games we broadcast, the more coverage we create, the more diversity we have—the more equity we can drive. The more investment we can generate, the more growth we can rightfully have.

That's why I, alongside Olympians and champions Sue Bird, Chloe Kim, and Simone Manuel, created TOGETHXR. We didn't want to wait any longer for others to decide our stories were worth telling. We would tell them ourselves. We believe that female athletes are incredible multi-hyphenates who move culture forward. Sports, after all, are not just a microcosm of culture. Sports *are* culture. And women's sports sit at every intersection.

This collection of diverse stories celebrates that central role of women's sports, and I am so proud to be a part of bringing this book to you.

This is for the female athletes who broke (and continue to break) barriers. Who blazed paths in the face of adversity for the generations to come. Who reclaimed their power. Who grew the game without diminishing their unique selves.

This is also for the generations who will be inspired to do the same.

We are in the margins no more.

I hope you love this collection as much as I do.

—Alex Morgan

9

INTRODUCTION

When I was growing up, my sport of choice was gymnastics. I memorized Olympians' floor music, papered my bedroom walls with pages of *International Gymnast*, and spent my weekends at endless gymnastics meets. I loved the sport, but I should be clear that I was not, by any stretch of the imagination, *good* at it.

I got so many positive things out of gymnastics, even though none of those things were a gold medal or even a score higher than 7.3. Through my participation in the sport, I developed greater poise, balance, strength, flexibility, and confidence. I gained a community of teammates and role models. I found the courage to try new skills, knowing I could (and likely *would*) fall, but believing that I would be able to get back up. By nature, I was a bookish, type A child, so none of this came naturally to me. I fought for it all because that's how much I loved the sport.

Now, decades later, I am—unsurprisingly—not a professional athlete. I work in book publishing, a field made up mostly of formerly bookish, type A children. When I was asked to develop a book publishing program for female sports–powered media and apparel company TOGETHXR, I knew I wanted to create books that would give readers the feelings that gymnastics had given me.

TOGETHXR is committed to amplifying women's voices and experiences, and with *Play It Forward* we aimed to do that across a broad range of athletes. With valuable input from researcher and journalist Lyndsey D'Arcangelo, we found stories of athletes from Iran to the Yucatán Peninsula to North Carolina, participating in sports from tennis to football to log rolling, as little girls and as senior women, on international stages and in their own backyards.

In compiling the list of stories, it was important to me that this book be not just about a few big stars. What athletes like TOGETHXR's founders Sue Bird, Chloe Kim, Simone Manuel, and Alex Morgan can do is remarkable—and way outside the realm of what most of us can even imagine accomplishing. So in *Play It Forward*, we wanted not only to celebrate the big names but also to showcase how participating in sports can have a positive impact on women's lives regardless of their level of fame or success. For the women in this book, sports have given them community when they were otherwise isolated, a voice when they were otherwise silenced, opportunities when they were otherwise limited, control when they were otherwise denied it.

It was also important to us that this book focus on telling modern-day women's stories. In our awareness of and admiration for women who changed sports history, it can be all too easy to overlook the women who are right now changing sport's future. Breaking boundaries isn't a thing of the past. It's ongoing.

Once I'd compiled a list of stories for this book—and trust me, there were so many more than we could fit in here!—I set out to find the right journalists to report and write them. The essays you're about to read come from eighteen talented female and nonbinary writers based all over the United States and the world. They used the power of their words to bring these athletes' stories to you. And I am so excited for you to read what they've written.

By the end of this book, I hope you'll understand—just as I did, when I was a young and not-very-good gymnast—that success doesn't always mean being the first or the only or the fastest or the strongest. Success also happens when you just keep playing, and you keep moving forward.

–Leila Sales, director of publishing, TOGETHXR

They Are Trailblazers

KATIE HNIDA AND THE WOMEN OF COLLEGE FOOTBALL

By Lyndsey D'Arcangelo

One fall evening in the late 1800s, a crowd of college-age men chattered around an open field, their voices loud and boisterous, their breath visible in the crisp air. Colored leaves covered the ground like a tattered quilt, spread across every inch of the faded green grass. The sun was setting and the sky was bursting grapefruit pink along the horizon. Ten women of a similar age, dressed in skirts and stockings, were split into two sides. Five sported the colors of Yale, the other five Princeton—both universities that women would not be allowed to attend as students for another seventy years.

Little did the crowd know, the women weren't there to prance around and look cute for the boys. They were there to play football and maybe even kick each other's asses, and they didn't care who was watching.

This women's football scrimmage took place at Sulzer's Harlem River Park on November 21, 1896. It was written about in New York City's the *Sun* and is said to be the first instance ever recorded of women playing football. At the time, everyone agreed that women were too fragile and demure to play sports. Male physicians then, and for decades after, deemed any sort of physical activity harmful to women and their reproductive organs (which were, of course, considered the most important part about them).

And football was on a completely different level. Women were far too delicate for such roughness and brutal physicality. They belonged at home, tidying up the kitchen, making endless sandwiches, and mending torn slacks. The game at Sulzer's Harlem River Park was meant to be a joke—a form of entertainment preceding a fancy-pants masked ball for the members of a men's uppity social club. But apparently, someone forgot to tell the women.

Once the ball was kicked, the players tore into each other with such fervor that the game turned into a fierce, physical, and scrappy rumpus. Before long, the cops were called to break up the game out of fear for the women's safety. Had the men not clutched their pearls, the scrimmage would have continued, and who knows what would have happened? Maybe the narrative of women's football history would have been written much differently. But instead, this one game remains a mere blip on the sports world's radar.

After football was invented in the 1880s, women were thwarted from playing it at every turn. Although recreational, gimmicky, and powder-puffy women's football events were continually held across college campuses in the following decades, they were never taken seriously or ever seen as legitimate football contests.

Then, with the passage of Title IX in 1972, the football door opened a crack. The '70s rolled into the '80s and then the '90s as girls dared to participate at the youth and high school levels—some making history in the process for being the first to do so at their school, at their youth

Women who wanted to play didn't *want* to play against men. They wanted their own teams and leagues.

organization, or in their respective state. Crowds gasped. Articles were written. Parents, depending on which side of the scoreboard they were on, cheered or sneered.

As time went on, women athletes and teams and leagues grew and evolved in other sports, particularly in basketball and soccer, and garnered some hard-earned respect. But women and football remained a quandary. Despite over one hundred years of societal evolution, the same stereo-typical concerns posed back in the late 1800s continued to circulate well into the next millennium: Women could get seriously hurt, they don't understand the game, football is too rough, it's too masculine, they aren't as strong, they don't know how to throw the ball or catch or kick, they can't physically compete with boys and men.

The irony is the women who wanted to play didn't *want* to play against men. They wanted their own teams and leagues and the opportunity to compete against one another. But since those didn't exist at the youth, high school, and college levels (the National Women's Football League, or NWFL, was the first women's professional football league of its kind and ran from 1974 to 1988), they had no other choice but to hop on the boys' and men's squads, and even then, only when given the chance.

Enter Katie Hnida.

Hnida attended Chatfield High School in Colorado and was a kicker on the high school football team. She played regularly, hitting three field goals and twenty-seven extra points on the season during her senior year, a feat that earned her a spot on *Teen People*'s America's Top 20 Teens list. In college, Hnida joined the Buffaloes as a walk-on placekicker at the University of Colorado Boulder.

Though Hnida suited up for Colorado games, she never saw the field and eventually transferred to the University of New Mexico. Again, Hnida made the football team as a walk-on placekicker. Only this time, she was given the chance to play. In August 2003, she kicked two extra points against Texas State University.

While Hnida isn't the first woman to play college football in the United States, she's the first to hit a notable benchmark at the Division I level: scoring points in a game at the highest level of competitive college sports.

But Hnida's achievements are only part of her story. There's an off-the-field dynamic that is often left out of the history books. The adversity Hnida endured on her quest to play football is more than anyone should have to bear in a single lifetime. Not only was she ridiculed and doubted for her skills on the football field, but she was also harassed and subsequently raped by a teammate in the locker room at Colorado. She was cast aside, dismissed, and told repeatedly she didn't belong. She was terrorized by a stalker. Teammates exposed their genitals to her as a gag. She was groped in team huddles. To this day, social media comments about Hnida's accomplishments are enough to make you want to punch a wall, or at the very least never look at Instagram again.

While at Colorado, Hnida courageously reported the harassment and incidents (not the sexual assault) to her head coach, Gary Barnett. He, unsurprisingly, did nothing to support her. Worse, he pled ignorance to all of it.

Barnett's tenure with the Buffaloes didn't end well. Other women lodged allegations of similar abuse, and he was exposed in a recruiting scandal before being ultimately forced to resign—getting a $3 million buyout in the process, so don't shed too many tears for him. He also maintained in a bitter and infamous quote: "It's obvious Katie was not very good. She was awful. Katie was not only a girl, she was terrible, okay? There's no other way to say it."

"That [quote] actually did not bother me that much," Hnida told Jemele Hill in an interview from an ESPN column in 2006, when she was twenty-five. "I thought it was kind of a classless thing to say. That was the guy I knew. But when it came down to them really actually going after my character trying to smear that, I was really naive about that too. I was aware they had tried stuff with the other women who had come forward. But I was thinking, *Okay, there is no alcohol involved in mine. I was a virgin when I was raped. I don't have much of a past that they can dredge up.* But stuff was made up, and that hurt more than anything. It just seems so inhumane to me. I can't believe somebody would do that to cover their own rear end, I guess."

Hnida's time at Colorado was harrowing. But she somehow found the strength to continue her dream of playing college football. This persistence led her to New Mexico, where acceptance and support were plentiful. She got to play, and she got to score. But the damage had been done, and kicking was never fully the same. Hnida details the entirety of her experience in her 2006 autobiography, *Still Kicking: My Journey as the First Woman to Play Division I College Football.*

It's important to note that Hnida's legacy isn't just about kicking (literally) down a door. It also brought the darker side of a male-dominated sport to light. It brought necessary awareness to what female athletes deal with just to be able to participate and play a sport they love. It made the path a little smoother for those who have followed.

And people *have* followed. During the Super Bowl LIII telecast in January 2019, Antoinette "Toni" Harris appeared in a Toyota commercial. After playing as a safety for two seasons at East Los Angeles College (ELAC), Harris was the first woman in history to be offered a college football scholarship in a full-contact (non-kicker) position from a four-year university. Harris received six total scholarship offers, including one from Central Methodist University, where she went on to graduate with honors in 2021.

The fact that Harris got her college football start at ELAC is fitting.

"When I was a student at ELAC in the early seventies, one of our female professors and coaches, Flora Brussa, went to Washington as part of a team to write Title IX. That law made it possible for our women's sports program to begin," said Rose Low, a former professional football player for the Los Angeles Dandelions of the NWFL. "When that door opened for us, who would have imagined that a female would play on the men's [football] team fifty years later and then be offered a scholarship to play at a four-year school? Maybe because a few of my schoolmates and I dared to play tackle football back then, a seed was planted for the women who followed to try."

Soon after Harris came Sarah Fuller, a goalkeeper on Vanderbilt University's women's soccer team, champions of the 2020 SEC Tournament. Fuller's senior year coincided with the Covid-19 pandemic. When Vanderbilt's football team's kickers couldn't play due to Covid exposure, Fuller was called in. She didn't know football, but she knew how to kick. She became the first woman to play and score in a football game in a Power Five conference.

In September 2023, Haley Van Voorhis secured her own place in the record books as the first woman to play in an NCAA game (Division III) in a full-contact position. Van Voorhis took the field for Shenandoah University for a single play, and the 5'4", 145-pound free safety held her own, even chasing down the quarterback.

"There's definitely people out there who see the story and think, *This girl's going to get hurt*," Van Voorhis told ESPN. "I hear that a lot. Or, 'She's too small, doesn't weigh enough, not tall enough.' But I'm not the shortest on my team, and I'm not the lightest."

It's not hard to look at Harris, Fuller, and Van Voorhis, as well as other women players at the college level, and connect the dots back to Hnida. But the truth is, their legacy goes back even further than that. Despite the many roadblocks and tall hurdles, women have been playing football in some way, shape, or form since the sport was invented.

If only the women who played that day at Sulzer's Harlem River Park could see all the amazing, talented, bold, fearless, and badass women's football players now, making the most of their opportunities to play, whether in women's football leagues, youth programs, flag football, coed two-hand touch, high school, or college.

They would be proud.

"ALL YOU CAN DO IS SHOW UP, BRING THE VALUE THAT YOU HAVE, BRING THE INTANGIBLES THAT YOU BRING, AND SEE HOW IT ALL FITS."

Sue Bird

They Build the Community They Need

INDIGENOUS WOMEN RUN

By Allison Torres Burtka

When Verna Volker started running in 2009, she didn't see many runners who looked like her—not at races or in the pages of running magazines. Most of the women pictured in there were thin, white, and blonde. Verna, who is Navajo and had given birth to three of her four kids by then, was none of the above.

Although she didn't see many Native women runners, Verna knew they were out there, all over the country, both on reservations and in urban areas, and she had connected with a few on social media. And so, in 2018, she created an Instagram account and Facebook page called Native Women Running.

Through this platform, Verna started sharing the stories of Native women from different tribes, living in different places, running for different reasons, and chasing different goals. They cheered each other on, and it started to feel like a community.

Now, the Instagram account has more than thirty-two thousand followers, and Native Women Running has expanded way beyond social media—it helps Native women get to races and supports them on the ground. And this is a big deal: The costs of travel, lodging, and fees limit who enters races. "A lot of our women, they travel from the reservations

Verna Volker

into the cities for races," and not everyone can afford that travel, Verna says. In the United States, Indigenous communities face disproportionately high rates of poverty.

Verna wanted to make it easier for Native women to show up, so Native Women Running has been partnering with race organizations to sponsor runners, create teams, and defray costs. So far, they've created about 30 teams across the country and supported about 150 women, either through teams or sponsorships.

When Verna started Native Women Running, "I didn't see myself in these spaces," she says. "We're the minority of the minority." Now, "Native women time and time again will tell me, 'I feel seen, I feel connected. It's nice to see someone that looks like me at these races and have someone there to support me.'"

"It's really created this sisterhood," Verna says. "Usually when we select these women, we have a group chat, and then they get to know each other, and then they meet each other at these events for the first time. And then after that, they have this experience that's really, really positive."

Native Americans are not a monolith, but running is central to some tribes' cultures. A Navajo coming-of-age ceremony for girls, for example, involves them running toward the rising sun. For many Native people, running is a form of prayer.

Running is "a spiritual connection to our roots" and to the land they're running on, Verna says. "We, as Native people, have historical, generational trauma," and running helps heal from that, she explains. "Running is medicine. It's our prayer, it's our healing."

Indigenous women face high rates of abduction, murder, and rape. The statistics for US women overall are horrific—27 percent have been raped in their lifetimes—and even worse for Native women. According to the Centers for Disease Control and Prevention, 43 percent of American Indian/Alaska Native women have been raped.

Each year on the fifth of May, which has been designated the national Missing or Murdered Indigenous Persons Awareness Day, Native Women Running and other organizations host runs and marches to raise awareness of the Missing and Murdered Indigenous Women and People (MMIW/MMIWP) crisis.

For Indigenous women, the MMIW crisis isn't abstract. When they run to honor people who have been murdered or gone missing, many are running for people they know personally. They run to raise visibility of a crisis that many non-Native people don't even know exists.

They also run to raise funds for the families of people who have been taken or for organizations supporting them. Such efforts "really honor their loved ones who have gone missing or who have been murdered—and honor the families who are tirelessly putting in the efforts to seek justice and hopefully healing in their lives," says Jordan Marie Whetstone, a Lakota woman who founded Rising Hearts, a collective that combines running and advocacy.

Rising Hearts' Running on Native Lands initiative works to make land acknowledgments a regular part of races. The initiative connects race directors with local Indigenous communities who are the traditional stewards of the land. It encourages the race organizations to support them beyond the land acknowledgment, such as by donating a portion of race fees to a local Indigenous youth group.

Both Native Women Running and Rising Hearts have also helped raise awareness of the boarding school system that forcibly assimilated generations of Native children. Many children were removed from their families and abused, and hundreds of their bodies have been found at school sites in the United States and Canada. Jordan says this crisis needs to be seen as connected to the MMIW crisis. Both are atrocious, and both have gone without much notice from the mainstream.

This kind of advocacy work is heavy. However, "There is joy in this really dark, heartbreaking reality that we're all part of, as advocates or as survivors, or as the family who is fighting for justice and seeking answers," Jordan says. "I think something that is really beautiful about Indigenous peoples is the resilience that is there. There is still joy, and I think that's what keeps us motivated and keeps us going and keeps us supporting each other and rooting for each other."

Jordan is a fourth-generation runner, and her grandfather is the one who introduced her to the sport. Now, running is a way of uniting with him. She says, "Running is where I truly feel most connected to my surroundings and most connected to my grandfather."

Jordan completed the 2019 Boston Marathon as a prayer run. She dedicated each mile to a different missing or murdered Indigenous woman or girl and ran with a red handprint over her mouth and the letters MMIW on her leg in red paint. "The red handprint symbolizes the voices that have been silenced by this epidemic in violence, and also it's the color that our ancestors see when they transition to the next phase in life," she says.

One Indigenous runner who noticed Jordan's Boston Marathon run is Rosalie Fish, then a senior at Muckleshoot Tribal School on the Muckleshoot reservation in Washington. Rosalie, a member of the Cowlitz tribe, asked Jordan if it was okay for her to adopt the handprint and MMIW in red paint. Jordan gave her the go-ahead, so she ran with paint in competition.

Rosalie thought this would be a one-time thing, and she didn't expect all the media attention that she got for running with red paint. "I just came to terms with the fact that, even if it wasn't my original decision to be this advocate or this spokesperson, that by getting this type of

Jordan Marie Whetstone

awareness or by having this platform, it's a privilege—and that I need to utilize it," she says.

So she went into advocacy mode, using her platform to represent her community and raise awareness of issues she cares about—including MMIW but also other challenges youth face. As a queer woman of color and a survivor of violence with PTSD, Rosalie knows what some of these challenges feel like. Beyond running with paint, Rosalie has been giving TED Talks and speaking at middle and high schools.

When Rosalie committed to Iowa Central Community College, she became the first student from her high school to sign a letter of intent for college sports. She later transferred to the University of Washington, where she earned her bachelor's degree in social work while running cross-country and track. Along the way, she's worked as an MMIWP family advocate intern with Mother Nation, a social services nonprofit for Native women. She also received the Women's Sports Foundation's Wilma Rudolph Courage Award.

The first time Rosalie spoke at a school, it was at her own, when she was a senior, shortly after her first time running with red paint. She spoke to middle school students and first-year students.

"I decided that I wanted to use that opportunity to speak about something a little bit less known. I had recently had a family friend who had been struggling with suicidal ideation. So instead of going up to talk about running for missing and murdered Indigenous women, or, you know, doing college classes or getting into the major that I wanted to or anything like that, I told them that people would look at my accomplishments and never would guess that I had started at that school surviving a suicide attempt," Rosalie says. The students heard her. "It was one of the first times that I saw a room of middle schoolers and young high schoolers, like, not looking at their phones or not talking. They were all just looking right back at me."

That reaction told Rosalie that if she's transparent and vulnerable with her story, she can have an impact on youth, especially "youth that might be in the same position that [she] was."

Speaking to younger teens became a passion. "It kind of became my goal to be the person that I needed to see when I was in that point of my life," Rosalie says.

Sometimes, when Rosalie visits students, they've prepared questions for her—and this is one of Rosalie's favorite parts of public speaking. "I get questions as intentional as 'What can we, as middle schoolers, do to help Indigenous people?' to other questions such as 'Pineapple on pizza—yes or no?'" she says. "And I am always just so touched by how these students are engaging in social issues and how they're able to connect to my story and vice versa."

Rosalie is a Brooks Run Happy advocate, which funds her visiting high school track teams—particularly tribal schools—and bringing each runner a free pair of Brooks running shoes. She loves doing this because it makes running more accessible to kids who might have a hard time affording high-quality running shoes—and also because it's fun to hang out with these teams.

The community of Indigenous runner-advocates is growing. "I think it takes one or two acts of courage from an Indigenous advocate or an Indigenous woman who is a runner, and it spreads," Rosalie says. That's what happened with her. "I was at first only an Indigenous runner, and then seeing Jordan Marie Whetstone and her courage put me on the path of advocacy."

One point of connection for many Native runners is the organization Wings of America, which empowers Native youth through running. For example, Rosalie says she ran on a Wings of America team with Navajo athlete Aliandrea Upshaw in high school, and later they competed at the same collegiate meets.

"I think something really special about these groups of Indigenous runners and Indigenous advocates is how tight-knit we are, and how heavily we impact each other," Rosalie says. "I think being an Indigenous athlete can be kind of lonely sometimes, so to be able to have found each other even though we're in different spots in the country is really special."

The community spans women of diverse backgrounds, levels of running experience, competitiveness, and age—Rosalie is in her early twenties, and Verna is fifty. It also includes Patti Catalano Dillon, a pioneer in women's running in general but especially for Indigenous women. She is Mi'kmaq. In 1980, she became the first American woman to break 2:30 in a marathon—plus she broke American and world records at several distances.

Patti told me as part of the Starting Line 1928 oral history project, "The Native-ness in me came out because I could run. I really attributed the running to the blood that I had, the high work ethic." When running, Patti explained, "I felt different than other people, meaning that it flows in you—the ancestry. . . . And when it's acknowledged or you do something, it ignites, and it just flows through you."

Now, Patti is head coach of Wings of America's Wings Elite Program for Native athletes.

Native women runners show up at races, sometimes drawing attention when running with red paint or wearing traditional ribbon skirts—and they represent their communities at races that may have few other Native participants.

A Native Women Running team ran the New York City Marathon for the first time in November 2023, after the organizers, New York Road Runners, invited them. "That means a lot to us," Verna says. "It was an incredible experience."

Before the opening ceremonies, New York Road Runners took a video of the Native Women Running team's very first in-person meeting. "All of us were dressed in our Native outfits—there's some of us who are from Navajo and from different tribes, and so we wore our Native dresses," Verna says. "And if you watch that video, you will see how we're crying."

The video shows Verna saying to the group, "You belong here."

"BEING STRONG IS NEVER EASY."

Serena Williams

They Never Stop Swimming

TWO FRIENDS TAKE LESSONS FROM THE WATER TO THE WORLD

By Lauren J. S. Porter

I spoke to Madeline Murphy Rabb and Ann E. Smith as rain stormed outside my window on a December day. The weather seemed fitting because they both love the water (though generally, they prefer it in swimming pools, not coming down from the sky). Five decades into their friendship, the two women dive into the deep end of pools. Madeline is seventy-eight. Ann is eighty-four. And they're competitive swimmers.

There's a long history of Black Americans being hesitant around the water. To this day, African American children are twice as likely as white children to not know how to swim. Perhaps some of that is due to the generational trauma of the Middle Passage. Surely lack of opportunity plays a huge role. In the days of segregation, when Black and white people in the United States were divided in every facet of life—schools, bathrooms, water fountains—of course access to swimming pools was unequal too. Fewer public pools were built in predominantly Black neighborhoods. Those pools that Black people *were* allowed to use were generally less appealing and more poorly maintained than their white counterparts.

But even all that deep-rooted hate couldn't stop the folks who flocked in droves to the freedom that the water brings—Ann and Madeline included.

For Ann, swimming was a form of exercise. And Madeline was taught to swim by her parents at an early age. Neither girl was competitive, but both enjoyed being in the water.

As young adults in the summer of 1966, they migrated to Chicago from their respective hometowns one month apart from each other; Madeline came from Wilmington, Delaware, in July, and Ann moved from Jefferson City, Missouri, in August. They settled into careers and communities that took them away from the pool lanes and into the professional world. Ann became the first African American full-time faculty member at Eastern Illinois University, and Madeline became the director of the Chicago Office of Fine Arts. One day their paths crossed, and a "hello" turned into a six-hour conversation that birthed a lifelong friendship. The next few decades brought them considerable professional success, and they both became dedicated to helping Black people expand their minds, their tastes, and their perception of possibilities.

Then retirement came floating by.

As the next phase of life approached, the same passions that helped them navigate the working world helped them in the water too.

First up was Ann. She decided that she wanted to live to be one hundred after her great-grandfather prophesied that for one of his own children. Ann determined that it was her destiny to keep the hope of her ancestors alive. She prescribed herself an elixir for long living: a combination of walking, biking, and, of course, swimming.

Ann had always been athletic. She did cheerleading in high school and college, enjoyed organized athletic competitions with a softball team called the BnB Bombers in her hometown, and had fun playing basketball, touch football, and kickball with friends. But because she graduated from college some twenty-two years before Title IX—the US civil rights law that offers protection from discrimination based on sex in federally financed education programs or activities—her participation in the games didn't carry the same weight as it would now. Something inside of Ann whispered that she had sports dreams worth exploring once her day-to-day wasn't filled with being a working woman.

One of those dreams was a triathlon.

Ann trained both physically and mentally for the endeavor. Picture it: A former professor turned director of marketing, then vice president of an insurance and consulting firm before becoming the first Black woman to hold elected office in Illinois, then being appointed associate chancellor at the University of Illinois Chicago and eventually president of the Gamaliel Foundation, now wearing a bathing suit, donning goggles, and diving headfirst into the water. She took to it immediately. Before Ann knew it, she'd completed eight triathlons and decided she still hadn't made the best of retirement.

"When I decided to be a triathlete, I was seventy; when I decided to do competitive swimming, I was seventy-four; and then at seventy-six, I decided to become a scuba diver; and I don't know what's next, but this has been an incredible experience," she said.

Now, look at yourself and think: *Have I done* anything *remarkable lately?* Then get ready to meet Madeline.

Madeline's grandfather was a physical education teacher at the then-all-Black Howard High School in Wilmington, where he created the very first swim team. He trained divers and swimmers, including Madeline's aunt, uncle, and mother. It was her mother and father who invested in Madeline's learning to swim. Swimming was part of her birthright; it was what flowed through her veins as she waded in the water of her grandfather's legacy.

After forty years building a life as a wife and mother, artist and arts administrator, plus jewelry designer, collector, and appraiser, too, Madeline made history as the first Black woman and professionally trained artist to be named the executive director of the Chicago Office of Fine Arts. She founded her art consulting business, Murphy Rabb Inc., where she built major African American art collections. And then, in her sixties, she returned to one of the things she loved most as a child: the water.

Madeline moved into a building with a pool, won a lesson with a swimming instructor, and connected with a trainer who could help her maintain her stride in the water. For the past fifteen years, this trainer has helped her reconnect with the passion of her family, and she has the ribbons to show for it.

Ann and Madeline believe in the joy, purpose, and serenity that life in the water can bring, no matter your age or level of experience.

"You can always improve, you can always learn something, and that's what I love about swimming. Because you think you know something and then you have a class or lesson and you'll get a breakthrough," Madeline told me, a smile beaming across her face.

One day in casual conversation, the same way that their friendship began, Ann mentioned that she'd won some medals in her new life as a competitive athlete. Madeline, having recently reconnected with her inner child–like self in the water, jumped at the chance to earn some medals too.

A week later, the pair drove from Illinois to Iowa for a regional competition in the National Senior Games, a league for adults over the age of fifty. Sure enough, soon after the games began, Madeline secured her very own gold and silver medals.

Since then, the friends have competed in any number of regional and national games. There's one word that Ann and Madeline use to describe their later-in-life endeavor.

"Badass!" they say with glee gliding through their voices.

"It's such a wonderful experience to be in the water, competing and winning, and I'd never had that. It was about me, competing against myself, and that's what I like about swimming," says Madeline. "When I'm in the water racing, I feel so powerful and there's nothing sweeter than that."

Ann echoes the sentiment. "Swimming for me has been like, there's no end. I can keep going, I can keep achieving, I can keep competing, and it's made me an even better leader."

She adds, "I'd always worked in social justice issues making sure that women [and] Blacks were included in higher education and the things that we were doing. I've always been working to make sure that people get what they deserve and that they're included. Who would have thought that swimming would be so meaningful? We've learned that we're still working in social justice."

Now it's happening in the water.

Remember when I said dating back to segregation, there was this thing with Black people and the pool? Well, this wasn't just some made-up, irrational phobia of the water. It was a designed tactic upheld by the white supremacy that divided this nation for years to keep Black children and adults from experiencing the joy that water brings.

In 1964, a motel manager poured muriatic acid into a swimming pool when two protesters, one Black and the other white, participated in a planned protest of the civil rights movement. The protesters were eventually dragged to jail by police. The motel management's disgusting act made headlines in St. Augustine, Florida, where it occurred, and the

"I can keep going,
I can keep achieving,
I can keep competing."

news traveled far and wide. Decades later, the infamous photograph of the act was printed in history books, which was how I learned as a child that people who looked like me weren't always welcome to swim freely in the public spaces I so openly enjoyed.

So what Ann and Madeline are doing now, years after life brought them together as friends who settled in the Windy City in the summer of 1966, has been in the works by the universe for far longer than either of them can fathom.

Their new lives as athletes have taken them to competitions across the country where they've become the top ten best swimmers in the nation at the Senior Games in their respective age groups. In 2023, in every regional Senior Games she competed in, Madeline won a combination of mostly gold and fewer silver medals in the 500-, 200-, 100-, and 50-yard freestyle and the 50-yard backstroke. Ann competed in and earned ribbons in the 50-yard backstroke and the 100-, 200-, and 500-yard freestyle.

They've even been celebrated at a film festival.

Team Dream is an eighteen-minute documentary that tells the story of their friendship, their relationship with the water, and their commitment to not letting anything—not even age—slow them down.

Directed by Luchina Fisher, the film won an Audience Choice Award at the Chicago International Film Festival and Best Documentary at the TIDE Film Festival, got them a standing ovation at the Tribeca Festival, and inspired the documentary's executive producer—who casually happens to be the Academy Award–nominated; Grammy-, Emmy-, and Golden Globe–winning actress, rapper, and singer Queen Latifah—to take up swimming once again.

When I asked the friends—whom unbeknownst to them, I'd mentally adopted as aunties throughout our forty-five-minute conversation—what they wanted their legacy to be, Ann put it plainly and Madeline couldn't agree more.

"I think that I want to be remembered as someone who felt there is no stopping. You don't arrive at a certain age and just sort of stop. There's so much more that you could achieve, and that you don't have to have a life that has just one focus. You can do a whole variety of things. You can just keep going. I want to inspire people to achieve their best and their most."

When my conversation with Ann and Madeline began on that December day, when pellets of raindrops adorned my window, I knew them to be two friends who became swimmers in retirement. By the time it was over, I learned that they are beyond the badasses they call themselves.

Ann and Madeline are not well-known rich and famous sports icons, legends, or GOATs whose names will be taught to every young athlete.

Who they are, however, are unsung freedom fighters who have defied the odds and paved the way, refusing to be limited by history and its slights by taking their strength from the water to the world. They are out here realizing the hopes of their ancestors, and reminding us all that dreams at any age are worth pursuing.

"I JUST NEED TO BE THE BEST VERSION OF MYSELF I CAN POSSIBLY BE."

Chloe Kim

They Find Strength in One Another

THE ATLANTA DREAM ENTER POLITICS— AND WIN

By Maitreyi Anantharaman

Players in the WNBA like to call themselves "the 144." It's a simple product of multiplication—twelve teams, twelve roster spots each—but one worn like a badge of honor. In all of American pro sports, there is no membership harder to earn. That number, 144, often feels unfairly small.

At the same time, the 144 demonstrate just how much power there is in a small number. A group of 144 can get together, grieve together, plan together, and act together. As Elizabeth Williams, who spent six seasons playing with the Atlanta Dream, once explained it, "We all know each other and we all talk."

The Dream are the WNBA's youngest franchise, named in tribute to a native son of Georgia and the radical dream he outlined on the steps of the Lincoln Memorial in 1963. The team's name also honors Atlanta as the birthplace of another dream. From the city's 1996 Summer Olympics emerged the idea of a women's professional basketball league in the United States. At that Olympic Games, Team USA recaptured the gold medal in women's basketball—a title the United States has not yet relinquished— and in doing so made the statement that the sport's long-invisible talent deserved a true platform.

Left: Atlanta Dream's Betnijah Laney and New York Liberty's Leaonna Odom and Paris Kea

For a decade, Angel McCoughtry was synonymous with the Dream. The franchise, then only two years into existence, drafted the 6′1″ wing with the first-overall pick in 2009. McCoughtry saw solutions on a basketball court that no one else did. She could enter space that looked impossible to maneuver, and then, somehow, dance her way to the rim. Blessed with a powerful first step, she was always finding the hidden angle, the hidden lane—always thinking one move ahead. The Dream had finished with a 4–30 record the season before they drafted her. Two seasons later, McCoughtry took them to the WNBA Finals. The night of Game 3, a prospective buyer for the club, Kelly Loeffler, sat courtside and watched the team's star sophomore set the single-game WNBA Finals scoring record.

So it was with some sadness that McCoughtry moved on from Atlanta when she reached free agency after the 2019 season. She still considered herself an ambassador for women's sports in the city, and she felt a sense of attachment to Atlantans—she had so badly wanted to bring them a championship. She even felt a sense of attachment to Loeffler, the businesswoman who ended up buying the Dream in 2011 and had been a mostly engaged, enthusiastic owner since.

Loeffler's wealth verged on caricature. The mansion she shared with her husband, naturally, had its own name, "Descante." The floors, naturally, were made of marble from Versailles. The fireplaces, naturally, had been imported from Cambridge, England. Once you've accumulated that much money, what else is there to do but buy a pro sports team?

When Georgia governor Brian Kemp looked at Loeffler, he saw an inoffensive white suburban woman, exactly the sort of voter Republican politicians had struggled to attract as Donald Trump became the face of their party. And so, in the summer of 2019, Kemp chose Loeffler to fill a vacant US Senate seat until an election could be held the following November.

"Here's what folks are going to find out about me," Loeffler said at Kemp's press conference to introduce her. "I'm a lifelong conservative, pro–Second Amendment, pro-Trump, pro-military, and pro-wall. I make no apologies for my conservative values, and I look forward to supporting President Trump's conservative judges. I am strongly pro-life. The abortion-on-demand agenda is immoral."

The 144, who speak out passionately against gun violence in their communities and express their anger at the notion of men politicizing women's bodies, were indeed finding out about Kelly Loeffler.

Later, McCoughtry would wonder about the Loeffler she had known and how real that version was. But something else was on McCoughtry's mind as Loeffler took office in early 2020. Although McCoughtry had grown up in Baltimore, Maryland, she was also a household name in Louisville, Kentucky, where she had been the University of Louisville's all-time leading scorer. And it was there in Louisville, in mid-March, that a twenty-six-year-old Black woman named Breonna Taylor was shot and killed by three Louisville police officers in a botched raid on her apartment.

McCoughtry and the rest of the 144 saw pieces of themselves in Taylor. How could they not? Their league was mostly composed of Black women; many of them were around Taylor's age at the time of her death. They lived very different lives—they were professional basketball players, while Taylor worked as an emergency medical technician—but they knew what it was like to be twenty-six. They knew what it was like to have a young woman's hopes and fears. Taylor's mother, Tamika Palmer, told the writer Ta-Nehisi Coates that her daughter was a good student, a little bossy, but a hard worker who loved her job.

Basketball is all about knowing when you have the leverage and knowing how to use it.

The WNBA season was scheduled to tip off a few months later, in a supposedly Covid-proof Florida "bubble" isolated from the rest of the country. Like some of their counterparts in the NBA, WNBA players struggled with the idea of basketball as usual. Several chose to opt out of the season—some for health reasons, others because they felt a calling to act in a summer of tumult.

The Dream's Renee Montgomery, a veteran of the league entering her eleventh year, was one of the players who chose not to play in the 2020 season. Her focus was everywhere but basketball. Protests and marches against police brutality had literally arrived at her doorstep in Atlanta. Gazing out her window one night, she called her parents and asked them for advice. Montgomery's mother was an HBCU professor with a keen sense for the sweep of history; she had lived in Detroit during the city's 1967 uprisings. "This is what people do when they don't feel heard," Montgomery's mother told her. Montgomery knew then that she had to be part of the movement. She took baby steps, handing out water at protests and paying attention to other activists, soaking up a new setting like she was a rookie again. She realized that if her heart wasn't in basketball, she owed it to her teammates to be where she wanted to be.

McCoughtry, meanwhile, still planned to play the 2020 season, and in June, with Palmer's blessing, she approached the league with an idea: The players would wear Taylor's name on the back of their jerseys. She mocked up a design, with *Breonna Taylor* printed on a thin, rectangular patch, right below her own name. WNBA players opened their season by dedicating it to Taylor. The 144 realized they had an opportunity to be "a voice for the voiceless," as Layshia Clarendon, then of the New York Liberty, said. They could use their platform to honor Taylor and every woman who had been a victim of racist violence.

Just before the season began, Loeffler realized she had an opportunity too. "I adamantly oppose the Black Lives Matter political movement," she wrote in a letter to WNBA commissioner Cathy Engelbert, urging Engelbert to thwart the players' plans. She was struggling in the polls against another right-wing challenger. "I believe it is totally misaligned with the values and goals of the WNBA and the Atlanta Dream, where we support tolerance and inclusion."

Montgomery reached out to Loeffler asking to have a conversation. *Could they just talk?* The message went unanswered. Clarendon, who had played for the Dream from 2016 to 2018, took Loeffler's letter as a kind of personal betrayal. They had dined in Loeffler's home and even introduced Loeffler to their wife. "I can't believe I ever stepped foot in Kelly's house and shared a meal with her. It's actually really hurtful to see her true colors," Clarendon wrote on social media. "Happy to own us as long as we stay quiet and perform."

How true *were* Loeffler's colors? Before she entered the world of politics, she had happily attended Dream games, never making a fuss when the league partnered with Planned Parenthood or when the team honored Democratic gubernatorial candidate Stacey Abrams at center court as part of the Dream's "Inspiring Women" initiative.

But now Loeffler was concerned with a different game. If she needed to score some points for the sake of her electoral prospects, well, she didn't mind throwing her team to the wolves.

No one understands power quite like a basketball player. It's the very basis of their game. The best can sense when the defender on them is smaller or slower and then attack accordingly. Basketball is all about knowing when you have the leverage—you might only have it for a split second—and knowing how to use it. No member of the 144 was as fabulously wealthy as Loeffler, whose husband was literally a billionaire. None of them lived in mansions with names or knew anything about Versailles marble. But the power they had was the power to organize, the power to speak with moral clarity and be heard. Loeffler might have owned their team. But she didn't own them.

The 144 met with an opponent of Loeffler's, a Democratic candidate for Georgia's senate seat named Raphael Warnock. A pastor at the Ebenezer Baptist Church where Martin Luther King Jr. once preached, Warnock hadn't been performing well in the polls. But over the course of two video calls, the players found someone who spoke to them. He answered their questions about issues that mattered to them—issues like reproductive rights and criminal justice reform. If Loeffler was unwilling to support the causes important to her team, then the team wasn't going to support her. The 144 was going all in on Warnock—and they were going to tell the world about him.

Sue Bird suggested T-shirts. Bird was one of the league's longest-tenured players and a member of the players union's executive committee. She had seen the 144 develop a voice for social justice; she had seen a time when the league's leadership was less comfortable with that voice. When Bird spoke, others listened. About a month after they met the candidate, she and other WNBA players showed up to their games wearing shirts that read "Vote Warnock."

They answered no questions about Loeffler. They wouldn't even acknowledge her. The #SayHerName movement saw the act of saying someone's name as a means of keeping them in the conversation, ensuring that a woman killed by police would never be forgotten. It followed that if the 144 didn't say Loeffler's name, they were refusing to hold the conversation on her terms.

Was there risk involved in defying a member of the league's ownership group? Sure. But the 144 believed that the risk was the point; it was how they would tell Georgia, and everyone else, that they were being sincere. To them, no concern mattered more than the concern of justice. Now it was up to the country to respond.

Within two days, the Warnock campaign had raised $183,000, much of it from 3,500 new grassroots donors. One political science researcher determined by examining Federal Election Commission data that the players' support for Warnock came at a pivotal moment and "changed the financial dynamics of the campaign." The late surge would give Warnock enough momentum to force a runoff election in January.

By the day of Georgia's special election, the Dream had dispersed. Most of them were competing in leagues overseas, where WNBA players often spend the offseason, supplementing their pay with a second job. Women's basketball players describe all kinds of experiences when you ask them about life abroad. Some feel the weight of isolation. Others cherish the thrill of being in an unfamiliar place. But all of them, whether they play in China or Spain, are made acutely aware of being American. They find they see their country more clearly when they leave it. "It's always been striking to me when I speak to my teammates from other countries about what it feels like to be Black in America," Elizabeth Williams recalled. McCoughtry had similar memories; someone overseas once asked her why Americans were so obsessed with division.

Williams lay awake in the middle of the night in Turkey, desperately refreshing her feed for good news from Georgia. She saw an update flicker across the screen. A few seconds later, the Dream group chat lit up. Her teammates were all up at odd hours around the world.

They had done it. Raphael Warnock would become Georgia's first Black senator. It was, for many of them, their most improbable—and most valuable—victory.

Loeffler's last shot—her craven attempt to make pawns of the 144— had clanked off the back rim. Clarendon, who had played in the NCAA Women's Final Four and the WNBA Finals, and knew something about high-stakes competition, confessed that there was something a little more special about flipping the senate: "Winning never felt so damn good."

"Winning never felt so damn good."

There's an epilogue, too, and a happy one. After she lost, it was back to Descante and its marble floors for Loeffler, who was now under increased pressure from players to sell her ownership stake in the team. Not quite two months after the election, the WNBA Board of Governors approved the team's sale to a three-member investor group. The first two members were business executives committed to keeping the Dream in Atlanta. The third was someone recently retired, a woman who had spent the summer learning how to mobilize others when the stakes are high and the world feels unyielding. Her name was Renee Montgomery.

She Keeps Climbing

FARAHNAZ IBRAHIMI FINDS A HOME IN SPORTS

By Lauren DeLaunay Miller

Every day before school, fifteen-year-old Farahnaz Ibrahimi would rise early in her home in Kabul, Afghanistan. She would roll out of bed, put on her team uniform, skip breakfast, and head out. On the ten-minute walk, she would have time to reflect on the impact of her actions. By walking through the doors to the martial arts training center, she was following in the footsteps of her brothers. She was learning to fight.

But she was also taking a risk. Men would taunt her outside the gym, bullying her with questions about what kind of parents would allow their daughter to bring them such shame—by participating in sports, in public. It was 2016, and Farahnaz had grown up in a time of relative stability for Afghanistan. Women, especially in cities like Kabul, had more rights and opportunities than they'd had in the previous generation. But conservative ideals still permeated most communities. Farahnaz worried that one day, the bullying could escalate into an acid attack or threats to the lives of her family members.

Farahnaz kept going, even as bruises accumulated on her face, winning competitions and refusing to concede to the idea that she didn't belong here. She mostly competed against other women, but sometimes she faced men too. Mixed martial arts was a rare sport in Afghanistan, especially for women, but Farahnaz was driven by the opportunity to prove that she could do something no one else in her community had done.

Sports became Farahnaz's escape. Not just MMA—she also started running, eager to explore her own personal limits. This, too, was rare, but she wasn't alone. Despite the ideologies of some, Farahnaz had a small community of other women athletes to practice with and compete against. Always looking for her next challenge, she instantly knew that a climbing program for girls called Ascend was for her when she heard her classmates talking about it.

The girls used strange lingo that Farahnaz didn't understand—top rope, lead—but that only made her more curious. Having reluctantly supported her martial arts and running, Farahnaz's parents lamented her ever-changing interests, but this time, she told them, was it. "This is the last sport I want to do," she told them. "This time you have to believe me."

Farahnaz quickly realized that being part of the Ascend team included more than just climbing instruction. The girls did yoga and fitness classes together, learned how to camp, and talked about leadership. Still, when the time came for her first trip to the mountains near Bamian, she was nervous. But her teammates—other mostly high-school-age girls from around Kabul—encouraged her, coaching her on how to relax, how to trust her feet and hands to carry her up the wall. By the time the trip was over, Farahnaz felt a new strength. Seeing a group of women lead this trip changed how she saw her country and her place in it.

"In Afghanistan, they use mountains as a place to fight," said Farahnaz. But when she went there for the first time, she thought to herself, *No, this is the place that I feel like I belong. This is the place that I feel safe. This is the place that I can change a nation.*

But that was before.

On August 15, 2021, following the dramatic withdrawal of US troops from Afghanistan, the Taliban seized power. "I couldn't believe it," said Farahnaz. One of five siblings, Farahnaz and her whole family gathered in their backyard. Life as they knew it was over.

The Taliban is an incredibly conservative political group, even by Afghan standards. And while they hadn't ruled the country in decades, their presence had continued to be felt in more rural parts of the country. There, women's opportunities for growth were slim. The group imposed harsh restrictions on women's lives outside of the home, especially on two things that were particularly meaningful for Farahnaz: school and sports.

Farahnaz's participation in these two things distinguished her among young Afghan women. While girls' education across the country had improved drastically in her lifetime, in 2017, Human Rights Watch reported that only 37 percent of high-school girls in Afghanistan were literate (compared to 66 percent of boys). Stigma, early marriage, and lack of resources have complicated girls' access to education across Afghanistan. The same is true for their participation in sports. But Farahnaz knew that, together, sports and schooling were giving her the tools to make a difference. From the time she was sixteen, she had been working with her mosque's imam to create a safe space to teach over one hundred girls in her community to read and write.

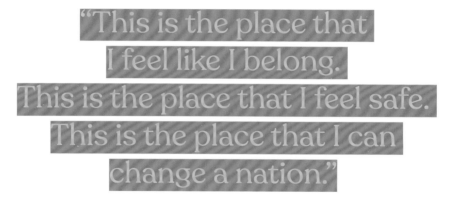

"This is the place that I feel like I belong. This is the place that I feel safe. This is the place that I can change a nation."

But that was over now. Before ever issuing a formal declaration, the Taliban's reign marked the de facto end of girls' education and participation in sports across Afghanistan. Scared of potential repercussions, and drawing on memories of how the Taliban had ruled during their last period of power, girls and women across the country became afraid to go outside. Their fears were soon validated: Within months of taking power, the Taliban would ban women and girls from both sports and middle and high school. Things around Farahnaz were changing quickly, but life itself had slowed to a crawl. She wrote in her journal that she had lost all hope. The brightness she saw for her future had gone dark.

While Farahnaz languished at home in Kabul, the United States–based staff of Ascend was hard at work. Overnight, their mission had pivoted from empowerment to evacuation. At a minimum, Ascend staff knew that their programming would cease to exist. In the worst-case scenarios, they worried that their girls could be punished for their involvement with Americans, sought out and harmed or sold as wives to Taliban members.

Two weeks after the Taliban takeover, Farahnaz was approached with an opportunity. Did she want to leave Afghanistan?

How, Farahnaz thought, could she possibly leave her country? This was her home. She wouldn't abandon it. And how could she leave her family? Ascend had limited space for evacuations, and their focus was on their team members, staff, and volunteers. But then: "My sister came to me and said, 'I wish I had this opportunity. Please, don't lose it.'"

While her decision to leave was quick, the process was anything but. Farahnaz put her trust in strangers, getting on a last-minute bus to Mazar-e-Sharif, a city in the northern reaches of Afghanistan. There, she was moved from wedding hall to wedding hall with hundreds of other hopeful Afghans, each awaiting their turn to board a plane to Qatar. For weeks, she and the other girls waited in large, loud rooms with no beds, little food, and hundreds of other people.

After weeks of waiting, the day finally came. But she wasn't done traveling yet. Once she made it out of Afghanistan, Farahnaz would spend more weeks at a refugee processing center in Qatar before eventually being transferred to the United States.

Ascend, who was organizing the evacuation of their participants, was also arranging homes that the girls could stay in once they reached the United States. In North Carolina, a group of Ascend volunteers banded together to create a "sponsor circle," a program that would allow everyday Americans to host refugees in their own homes. For the Ascend girls, this had the added benefit of keeping them close to one another. By the end of 2021, after months of uncertainty, Farahnaz arrived in North Carolina, ready to start her life anew.

Despite being commonly referred to as refugees, Farahnaz and the vast majority of Afghans who fled to the United States in late 2021 are not legally classified as such. Because of the expedient nature of their evacuation, most were given a temporary status known as humanitarian parole. While refugee processing can take years, this was a tool the Biden administration had to process and resettle Afghans quickly (they would do the same for many Ukrainians just a few months later).

Humanitarian parole let Farahnaz and her Ascend teammates access many of the things they would need to start new lives in the United States. They could go to school, get driver's licenses, and receive health insurance and financial assistance. Most importantly, it let them exist, legally, while they got their feet on the ground. But as Farahnaz would soon learn, the two-year limit on her parole status would come quickly. In between applying for college, learning to drive, and looking for work, she needed to find a long-term solution.

For most of the seventy-seven thousand Afghans who were granted humanitarian parole, the most straightforward path to permanent residence is asylum. For Farahnaz, this meant finding a lawyer, filling out mounds of paperwork, completing an eight-hour interview, and waiting for nearly a year as her case was decided by immigration officials. All this was made more complicated by the rushed nature of her evacuation and the current restrictions placed by the Taliban. Farahnaz's school records were difficult to obtain, for instance, because her school had closed. Asylum proceedings in the United States rely on an applicant being able to prove their story, and for Farahnaz, that proof was elusive.

College applications were another source of trouble for Farahnaz's path toward fulfilling her goals in her new country. Humanitarian parolees should be eligible for federal student aid, but the application, once again, requires documentation and assumes a reliance on the applicant's parents' participation. In North Carolina, where Farahnaz was living, parolees can't access in-state tuition because they are not permanent residents, which meant applying to more private schools with, hopefully, more funding opportunities.

Adapting to life in the United States felt like roadblock after roadblock to Farahnaz, but one thing provided an outlet for her to express herself and forget, at least momentarily, all she was up against. The Ascend volunteers who were hosting Farahnaz and the other Ascend participants were climbers, too, and they took Farahnaz and her friends to weekly sessions at the climbing gym and weekend trips to nearby cliffs. On the rock, Farahnaz could focus on the present. She could look at how far she had come and remember that climbing had given her the strength—and opportunity—to go on.

It wasn't only the act of climbing that helped Farahnaz settle into her new life, though. It was also the community. "It's wonderful," she said. "It's not just about the climbing; it's about supporting you mentally." American climbers stepped up to support her, providing a network she realizes many newcomers don't have when they arrive in the United States. As much as they helped her adjust, though, Farahnaz's temporary legal status hung over her.

The two years of Farahnaz's parole status came and went, and while she was able to extend it for another two years, more parole also meant more waiting and more uncertainty. "Do I belong to Afghanistan? No," said Farahnaz. Despite how much she missed it, she had left Afghanistan behind. "Do I belong to the United States? No." Farahnaz was feeling what many parolees describe as limbo. The lack of permanent residency left Farahnaz feeling lost in the middle, stuck between two countries.

But there was one place that Farahnaz felt at home. "The only place I always felt I belonged was the mountains."

Just over two years after arriving in North Carolina, Farahnaz's asylum application was approved. With that, she became eligible for permanent residency. Eventually—hopefully—she could use her permanent status to bring her family over to the United States to join her. She also started college, a dream she'd held ever since her days of teaching girls to read in her neighborhood mosque.

Around the same time, Farahnaz also took her climbing to the next level. She learned to lead, which meant that instead of relying on another climber to protect her, she could put the rope up herself and establish the route for others. Learning to lead on the rock in North Carolina reaffirmed to Farahnaz that she could continue to pave the way for Afghan girls, despite being so far away from the mountains of Bamian.

As she takes a break from her ascent, resting against the rock of North Carolina's Blue Ridge Mountains, Farahnaz can look out over the world. She can see how far she's come. For a moment, she just breathes, taking in the beauty of the view. And then, she keeps climbing.

Farahnaz Ibrahimi

They Fight Discrimination

BARING IT ALL FOR TITLE IX

By Frankie de la Cretaz

On June 23, 1972, President Richard Nixon signed Title IX into law, prohibiting sex-based discrimination in federally funded schools. The now-famous piece of legislation is often associated with women's sports, though athletics were not originally included in the bill itself. Nonetheless, sports very quickly became ground zero for the anti-discrimination law's application—and the place where Title IX would have some of its most visible impact.

But while Title IX is credited with major strides toward equality for women and girls in sports, its application was anything but seamless—or enthusiastic—when it came to universities providing their women's teams with equal opportunities, equal funding, or equal facilities. In fact, Title IX was mostly lip service after it was signed into law—until the Yale University women's crew team launched a revolutionary protest that landed them in the *New York Times* and Yale in hot water.

With a stripped-down, five-minute action in the office of the school's director of athletics, the 1976 Yale women's rowing team would become the face of Title IX and would empower generations of gender-marginalized athletes to demand what was rightfully theirs.

Title IX was modeled on parts of the 1964 Civil Rights Act and was designed to address the issue of women being denied entry into various educational institutions, not just as students but as faculty and scholarship recipients as well. Often referred to as "37 words that changed everything," the bill declares that "[n]o person in the United States shall, on the basis of sex, be excluded from participation in, be denied the benefits of, or be subjected to discrimination under any educational program or activity receiving Federal financial assistance."

While sports are not mentioned in the original text of the bill, athletics soon became a major focus of the discussion around Title IX when Congress asked the equivalent of today's Department of Education to address the practicalities of the law's application, including issuing regulations and guidance on women and girls in sports. For its part, the NCAA fought to limit Title IX's application to sports, fearing it would jeopardize their men's sports programs—and therefore their income streams. To this day, the NCAA itself is not liable for Title IX regulations, though its federally funded member organizations are.

When Title IX became law, there were some changes that happened immediately. Physical education in elementary and high schools, for example, became desegregated. But at the university level, change was slow—and not always a priority for school athletic programs. Some women

Yale women's crew team

were tired of asking nicely for their newly established constitutional rights to be upheld.

When the Massachusetts Institute of Technology women's crew team went varsity in 1974, they had nothing. "We used the leftover men's boats," team coxswain Roseanna Means said in an interview for the Margaret MacVicar Memorial AMITA Oral History Project. "We used leftover men's equipment. We used leftover men's sweats. There was no locker room for the women. The janitor had a closet that had a toilet in it. I think we might have used that." When the university refused to provide them with new uniforms, they got creative. The team decided to purchase their own "uniforms"—matching Mickey Mouse shirts and hats from Walt Disney World. That team eventually succeeded in lobbying to have a women's locker room installed as well.

Another crew team took their protest up a notch. Despite the directive from Title IX that women's and men's teams have equal access to facilities, the two crew teams at Yale could not have been in more different circumstances. After practices at the Robert Cooke Boathouse, a school bus would drive the athletes back to campus. But the women, who had just spent hours sweating and being sprayed by river water during their workout, had nowhere to shower until they got back to Yale. The men had a functioning locker room at the boathouse; meanwhile, all the women had was a small trailer with four showerheads—and even that was of no use to them. The university was in disagreement with the municipality of Derby regarding jurisdiction over the boathouse sewer line, so the hot water in the women's trailer wasn't hooked up.

Cold, wet, and smelly, the women huddled together on the bus waiting to head back to campus while the men washed the stench of practice off their bodies. In February of 1976, junior Anne Warner came down with pneumonia. Despite repeated pleas from the women for access to showers down by the Housatonic River, nothing changed. This culminated in an event that ESPN would later call "The Boston Tea Party of Title IX," with a leader whom Senator John Kerry would refer to as the "Rosa Parks of Title IX."

On March 3, 1976, nineteen members of the Yale women's crew team entered the office of Joni Barnett, director of women's athletics and physical education, wearing their navy-blue team sweats. They had arranged for David Zweig, the executive editor of the *Yale Daily News* and freelancer for the *New York Times*, to meet them there. He brought along a photographer, a freshman named Nina Haight. The two followed the athletes into Barnett's office. Then Haight climbed onto a desk and Zweig sat with his back to the women, both ready to document what happened next.

Led by their team captain, senior Christine Ernst, and team swing Warner, the women removed their clothing, revealing the words *TITLE IX* written on their naked bodies. Ernst read a short statement that the team had prepared. "These are the bodies Yale is exploiting," she began. "We have come here today to make clear how unprotected we are, to show graphically what we are being exposed to."

In the nude, the athletes laid out their case: The rain froze on their skin during practice, and then they were forced to sit on a bus for up to an hour as the ice melted into their clothes and mixed with the sweat that had already soaked the clothing they wore underneath.

"No effective action has been taken and no matter what we hear, it doesn't make these bodies warmer, or dryer, or less prone to sickness," Ernst continued. "We are not just healthy young things in blue-and-white uniforms who perform feats of strength for Yale in the nice spring weather; we are not just statistics on your win column. We're human and being treated as less than such."

The story ran the following day on the front page of the second section of the *Times* under the headline "Yale Women Strip To Protest a Lack Of Crew's Showers." Its impact was immediate: Within days, the hot water had been turned on in the trailer down by the river. The following year Yale added a women's locker room to the boathouse. Three years later, in 1979, the team went on to win the national championship.

That simple but daring act by the Yale rowers empowered legions of female athletes to demand more from their schools. And the universities themselves, seeing how humiliating the incident had been for Yale, feared similar disruptions from their own student athletes and took preemptive steps to implement the required changes. Would it have been preferable for them to be motivated by a genuine interest in equality, a sincere desire to do right by their students? Of course. But, hey, if you can't change The Man's attitudes, at least change his actions.

To this day, there are many high school and collegiate female athletes who must fight for their Title IX rights, just as the 1976 Yale crew team did before them.

Yale women's crew 1976 team captain Chris Ernst

One high-profile battle includes Lia Thomas and other trans athletes. In March of 2024, a group of more than a dozen current and former college athletes sued the NCAA, accusing the organization of violating their rights under Title IX by allowing Thomas, a transgender woman, to compete in the women's division in swimming. They alleged that transgender girls should be kept out of women's sports in order to "protect" cisgender athletes.

It was Title IX that unwittingly codified sex segregation into law when it came to organizing sports, as well as making biological differences in athletes' bodies a lynchpin of the anti-discrimination legislation. (It is worth noting that while Title IX itself permits sex-segregated sports, the courts have overwhelmingly suggested that the equal protection clause in the US Constitution does not.)

The warping of Title IX, an anti-discrimination law, into something that allows for anti-trans bad actors to push for discrimination against transgender students under the guise of "activism" goes against the very spirit of what those earlier activists fought so hard for. Former NCAA athletes and current WNBA players Layshia Clarendon and Brianna Turner have publicly advocated for trans athletes to be allowed to compete.

"This legislation is just a way to honor those people who worked hard to get Title IX," Wendy Schuler, a lawmaker in Wyoming who sponsored an anti-trans bill, told the *Los Angeles Times*. "For 50 years we've had the opportunity to compete as females and I just would hope we continue that fight."

Lindsay Parks Pieper, PhD, associate professor of sport management at the University of Lynchburg and the author of *Sex Testing: Gender Policing in Women's Sports*, told *YES!* magazine that the current push to weaponize Title IX as a means of excluding transgender women and girls from women's sports is "such a misrepresentation" of the legislation and the intent behind it.

Thomas is not the only modern athlete who has had to fight to protect her constitutional rights. In 2023, thirty-two female University of Oregon athletes filed a Title IX lawsuit against the school, alleging that the school treats its men's teams far better than its women's teams. The plaintiffs included members of the women's beach volleyball and women's rowing teams, and among their complaints were that the men's teams get higher quality equipment and facilities.

According to the lawsuit, Oregon's men's teams receive sport-appropriate gear that is tailored to each athlete, while the women's beach volleyball team receives gear at the beginning of the season, much of it used and ill-fitting, forcing players to borrow equipment from other teams or purchase their own out of pocket. In addition, the women's beach volleyball team alleged that it does not have its own designated locker room or practice and competition court on the school's campus, instead practicing at a nearby public park where the athletes have to rake the sand themselves to clear it of trash, animal feces, and drug paraphernalia. Not only that: The bathroom stalls at the park where the team practices do not have doors.

In 2022, former students from James Campbell High School, the biggest public high school in Hawai'i, filed a landmark sex discrimination case under Title IX, alleging widespread disparities in the way girls' and boys' teams were treated at the school. While the boys had dedicated locker rooms and practice spaces, the girls had to lug their equipment around the school with them all day. The girls' water polo team was forced to practice in the ocean, battling waves and wildlife, because they didn't have access to a pool.

Women athletes are using Title IX to target financial aid and scholarship distribution too. In 2022, a group of current and former female NCAA athletes filed a Title IX lawsuit alleging unequal distribution in financial aid. The former athletes argued that San Diego State University provided financial aid to male athletes at a disproportionate rate—in the two academic years prior to the complaint, the school provided female athletes with $1.2 million less in athletics financial aid than it did to their male counterparts. The result of this discrepancy is that, for many women who are part of the 6 percent of high school athletes talented enough to make a collegiate team, they may not even be able to play because they can't afford to attend college.

If there's one thing women athletes have proven throughout history, it's that they won't go down without a fight. That spirit is alive and well, even though it shouldn't have to be. The real fight is one with an eye toward inclusion—not exclusion. Take it from some of the original pioneers of Title IX activism. "That kind of stuff is still happening," Ernst, one of the architects of the 1976 Yale rowing protest, told ESPN in 2012. "That's why we have to keep fighting."

They Are Mothers

ATHLETES DEMAND MORE MATERNITY RIGHTS

By Frankie de la Cretaz

Serena Williams won the Australian Open while pregnant—and then almost died while giving birth. Olympians had to fight the International Olympic Committee to let them bring their breastfeeding infants to the 2020 Tokyo Games with them. Allyson Felix had to publicly challenge Nike to stop them from cutting her pay when she returned to the track postpartum. And Icelandic professional soccer player Sara Björk Gunnarsdóttir had to take legal action to receive her salary while pregnant.

Elite athletes do incredible things with their bodies—the strength, skill, endurance, and control they can achieve is nothing short of remarkable. But for elite athletes who are birthing mothers, their bodies also do something incredibly human and, in many ways, quite ordinary. You know what else is quite ordinary? The sexism and discrimination that birthing athletes experience when it comes to exercising their reproductive rights.

For many years, having a baby was a career-ending endeavor for a woman athlete. But as more opportunities to play women's sports at elite and professional levels become available, playing careers have lengthened, and so many more women are giving birth while still actively pursuing an athletic career. Unfortunately, the protections those new parents need to care for their bodies—which are a necessary part of their jobs—and their

Left: Alysia Montaño

babies have not yet materialized in so much of the sports world. Which means the athletes are fighting for them.

"Getting pregnant is the kiss of death for a female athlete," Phoebe Wright, who was a runner sponsored by Nike from 2010 through 2016, told the *New York Times* in 2019.

From a scientific or medical perspective, it absolutely does not need to be that way. In 2015, the International Olympic Committee put together a panel of experts to analyze the research around athletes' bodies during pregnancy and after childbirth. They released a report in 2016, finding that it's safe for women to continue training during pregnancy as long as they adapt as their body changes.

Even still, athlete–mothers are having to fight for their ability to be both of those things at once without losing their jobs and livelihoods, or without putting themselves at great physical risk. From pregnancy to maternity leave to ongoing parental supports, the sports world is severely lacking the necessary protections to ensure that women are treated fairly when it comes to reproductive health and justice. In that way, professional athletes are in solidarity and community with women in nearly every other profession.

Professional athletes are in solidarity and community with women in nearly every other profession.

Much of the current push for maternity benefits in sports can be traced to a watershed moment in 2019 when three track athletes—Alysia Montaño, Kara Goucher, and Allyson Felix—went public in the *New York Times* about their experiences with Nike financially punishing sponsored athletes who had given birth, often pushing them back to competition before their bodies were ready.

In response to the public outcry, Nike amended their contract to state, "If ATHLETE becomes pregnant, NIKE may not apply any performance-related reductions (if any) for a consecutive period of 18 months, beginning eight months prior to ATHLETE's due date. During such period NIKE may not apply any right of termination (if any) as a result of ATHLETE not competing due to pregnancy." In other words, Nike could no longer stop sponsoring an athlete because she had the audacity to use her body for something other than sports.

And it wasn't just Nike—after the runners published their op-ed pieces, other brands like Athleta, Burton, and Brooks rushed to either add or share mom-friendly policies in their sponsorship contracts. Other athletes spoke out in support of the track athletes who had come forward. Some named sponsors who had been especially supportive of their pregnant athletes.

"For us, we've been fortunate that our primary sponsorship arrangement is with Comcast NBCUniversal, which fully supported us financially—and even accommodated our special needs—during our pregnancies," wrote twins and Olympic gold medalists Monique Lamoureux-Morando and Jocelyne Lamoureux-Davidson of the US women's hockey team with MSNBC. "The issues raised by the Nike story go beyond corporate sponsorship of athletes. For the two of us, and for millions of other working women, that story crystallized the importance of maternity benefits—for all working women, including athletes."

The Women's Tennis Association (WTA) changed their player ranking policy following Serena Williams's experience of leaving the league ranked No. 1 but returning to competition as an unseeded player following her time off for pregnancy, birth, and postpartum recovery. Giving birth had been a harrowing ordeal for Williams, who nearly died from blood clots after delivering her baby. Can you imagine: Serena Williams—winner of twenty-three Grand Slams, four-time Olympic gold medalist, one of the most successful athletes in history—showing up to a tennis tournament and being treated like she's nobody? The WTA's updated policy would allow a player who is out of competition due to a medical condition or pregnancy up to three years to use a "special ranking" without being penalized for their absence from the sport.

All these changes make it easier for moms to continue to compete at the highest level. The US Women's National Team's 2023 soccer training camp included five mothers: Alex Morgan, Crystal Dunn, Casey Krueger, Adrianna "AD" Franch, and Julie Ertz. But even while many leagues and companies are putting policies in place to rectify the problem, barriers persist.

Consider the collective bargaining agreement (CBA) the WNBA put in place in 2020, which guaranteed athletes fully paid maternity leave for the first time in league history and workplace accommodations for nursing players. It looks good on paper, right? However, in 2023, two WNBA players accused the league of pregnancy-related discrimination. Dearica Hamby filed a discrimination lawsuit against the Las Vegas Aces, alleging that the team retaliated against her once they found out she was pregnant, "caus[ing] the work environment to become unreasonably abusive and hostile." And Skylar Diggins-Smith claimed that she was denied access to the training facilities and team resources while on maternity leave from the Phoenix Mercury. This is especially frustrating for a player like Diggins-Smith, who had to hide her first pregnancy from her team in 2018 due to unsupportive league policies and would have hoped the new CBA would offer greater protection.

In 2021, Icelandic soccer player Sara Björk Gunnarsdóttir discovered she was pregnant while playing for Lyon, the renowned French professional team. Gunnarsdóttir says the team was supportive at first, but when she returned to Iceland to finish out her pregnancy at home, she stopped receiving paychecks from the club. Eventually, she had to report the team to FIFA—who indeed found Lyon to be in violation of policy—in order to access the money she was owed. Her time with the team came to an end as a result of their lack of both emotional and institutional support throughout her pregnancy—and when she returned to the team with her baby in tow. "This is not 'just business,'" Gunnarsdóttir wrote in the Players' Tribune. "This is about my rights as a worker, as a woman and as a human being."

"Change is not linear: It is often a jumbled mess of gains and losses, repetition and throughlines," Amira Rose Davis, an assistant professor in the department of African and African diaspora studies at the University of Texas at Austin, wrote for Global Sport Matters in 2023. "The increased support for athlete moms shows that we are in the midst of a new dawn in women's sports while the lingering challenges illuminate the barriers still standing in the way of progress."

Another lingering challenge? The rights of breastfeeding mothers, which were thrust into the international spotlight in 2021 in the lead-up to the (Covid-19-postponed) 2020 Olympic Games in Tokyo. Because of the ongoing coronavirus pandemic, athletes were not allowed to bring their families with them into the bubble of the Games, a restriction that included nursing infants.

This is not a new challenge, of course. Shortly after giving birth to her son in 2010, former Olympian Kara Goucher was forced by her doctor to make a choice between continuing to breastfeed and running 120 miles per week; there was no way her body could do both. She chose running, because she felt she had to return to competition in order to have her sponsorship payments from Nike resume. What's better for a newborn and their family: a mother who can breastfeed or a mother who can get paid? It's a question with no good answer. Here's a better question: Why is anyone being forced to make that choice?

A decade later, nursing mothers were being faced with the same impossible choice, albeit in different circumstances. Regardless, it seemed like the accommodations that athlete moms might need are a last consideration for the male-dominated organizations in charge of most organized elite sports.

Facing the International Olympic Committee's restrictions, Canadian basketball player Kim Gaucher said she was "forced to decide between being a breastfeeding mom or an Olympic athlete." And while well-meaning people tried to help find solutions by suggesting mothers try to pump a large supply of milk before the Games, Gaucher explained that athletes' bodies (and, honestly, pretty much all people's bodies) can't work that way: "I don't have enough milk in me to train as a high-level athlete, get my butt back in shape, *and* feed [my baby] currently, all while stocking twenty-eight days' supply."

Eventually, the International Olympic Committee was forced to amend their policy to allow nursing infants to attend the Tokyo Games with their mothers. Even still, the new policy was a logistical nightmare. Because children would have to stay at an off-site hotel, Spanish artistic swimmer Ona Carbonell ended up having to travel to Japan without her baby despite her technically being allowed to bring him.

"They wouldn't be allowed to leave the hotel room during the twenty-ish days I'd be in Tokyo," Carbonell said. "For me to go and breastfeed Kai whenever he needs it during the day I would have to leave the Olympic villa, the team's bubble, and go to their hotel, risking my team's health."

Clearly, support for mothers is lacking around the world, but it's particularly lacking in the United States. Employers are required to provide twelve weeks of maternity leave under the Family and Medical Leave Act, but that leave is not required to be paid. And of course this law does nothing to help mothers who are self-employed or gig workers—a category that many athletes fall into. In fact, in a 2019 study from UNICEF, the United States ranks last among forty developed countries when it comes to paid parental leave—it was the only Organization for Economic Co-operation and Development (OECD) country to offer zero federally mandated paid weeks of maternity leave.

The fact that working mothers are already not seen as entitled to benefits, combined with the societal framing of women athletes as "superwomen," means that the limitations of their bodies are perhaps even less considered than those of women in other fields. Despite the fact that an athlete's body is the tool she uses to perform her job, and therefore she needs to care for it in every way she can, the safety of athlete–mothers when it comes to their reproductive health seems to be an afterthought in the world of sports—even in leagues composed entirely of women.

"Right now, we don't treat pregnancy as something that's worthy of care," Letisha Brown, assistant professor of sociology at Virginia Tech, told Global Sport Matters in 2021. "This narrative of unbreakability is harmful because humans are breakable. By always focusing on them as being superhuman, it takes away from their actual humanity and their vulnerability to injury and pain and suffering."

Athletes will continue to fight for their reproductive rights, as evidenced by the fact that their persistence is the sole reason why any of those rights have been granted to them thus far. But they shouldn't have to fight so hard. The constraints of a world bound by patriarchal and capitalist ideals should not be uncritically applied to sporting institutions that cater to women athletes. In doing that, the athletes will always be at a disadvantage, fighting against cultural beliefs that lead to concrete policies that were not made with them in mind.

"THE ONLY THING I HAVE TO PROVE IS TO MYSELF ... THAT I CAN GET OUT THERE AND DO IT AGAIN."

Simone Biles

She Speaks Her Truth

DARIA KASATKINA AND THE POLITICS OF SEXUALITY

By Camber Scott-Clemence

I grew up in dusty West Texas, in a town where churches outnumber trees. A town that wears the title "Second-Most Conservative City in the Nation" like a badge of honor. The first-most conservative city was Provo, Utah, but I promise you—my hometown gives them a run for their money. It's a town that champions abstinence-only sex education while boasting some of the highest rates of teenage pregnancy and STDs. A town that is the buckle of the Bible Belt, where slurs and hate speech spit from mouths like an unpleasant taste. In a town like that, especially in the 1990s—when I was a kid—you quickly learn to conform.

For years, I adhered to the script. I married a man, had two children, and drove a minivan. To be honest, the minivan remains a lingering source of shame. A few years later, I was divorced and in therapy, embarking on a journey of self-discovery, shedding the layers of compulsive hetero-sexuality. Today, I proudly fly a Pride flag at my house, hold my partner's hand publicly, and advocate for LGBTQ+ rights. However, the journey to this point was fraught with fear and anxiety. Growing up in a town where being different was deemed unacceptable, I understood safety was found in hiding.

This was my experience in the United States, a country purportedly built on life, liberty, and the pursuit of happiness. But even here, as we face anti-LGBTQ+ policies like "Don't Say Gay" and bans on gender-affirming care, nothing can compare to the challenges confronting queer people in a country like Russia, where your very existence could have you imprisoned. And that is what makes the story of Daria Kasatkina all the more remarkable.

A top-ranking Russian tennis player, Daria bravely came out in an interview with blogger Vitya Kravchenko in July 2022. While I hesitate to compare West Texas to Russia—a country that ranks so low on the ILGA-Europe list that only Turkey and Azerbaijan fall below it—her story resonates deeply with me. When I look at Daria—or Dasha, as she prefers—I see someone who has also had the experience of growing up in environments hostile to a fundamental part of her identity.

When Dasha publicly declared her sexuality, the news reverberated across major media outlets. CNN, the *New York Times*, ESPN, *USA Today*, and the *Washington Post* reported on her story. Whether intended or not, Dasha became a symbol of resistance. Her decision to come out and to advocate for the LGBTQ+ community transcends the boundaries of sport, reaching into the hearts of a global community grappling with negative perceptions, oppressive laws, and deeply ingrained prejudices.

"This notion of someone wanting to be gay or becoming gay is ridiculous. I think there is nothing easier in this world than being straight," said Dasha. "Seriously, if there is a choice, no one would choose being gay. Why make your life harder, especially in Russia? What's the point?"

Dasha was born in Tolyatti, Russia, and started tennis at six after being influenced by her brother Alexsandr, who had played casually. Initially, she practiced two or three days a week. When they recognized her talent, her parents, Tatyana Kasatkina and Sergey Kasatkin—nationally ranked athletes in Russia in athletics and ice hockey, respectively—allowed her to compete at higher levels.

Excelling as a junior, Dasha won the Euro Under-16s Championship and a junior Grand Slam singles title at the 2014 French Open. She quickly climbed the rankings in her professional career, reaching #32 while only eighteen years old, securing her first Women's Tennis Association title at the Charleston Open in 2017. Her biggest career titles include the Kremlin

Cup and the St. Petersburg Trophy. In 2018, the same year she won the Kremlin Cup, Dasha was ranked #10 in the world.

However, Dasha had a challenging 2019. She ended the year far from where she began, dropping to #70. Things didn't improve in 2020, and Dasha finished the year ranked #72. As a result, she lost her Nike sponsorship and a fair bit of love for the game.

Dasha admits that the stress and expectations became too much, culminating in a mental breakdown in her hotel room. She locked her door and cried for two days straight.

"I was in a very bad state of mind, and I just didn't want to continue playing . . . the pressure, the nerves, the anxiety. We broke into the top ten earlier than anybody expected, and I just freaked out," explained Dasha. "I felt like I was in the middle of the sea and [had] forgotten how to swim."

The pressure to succeed stemmed from her childhood in Tolyatti. Following the collapse of the Soviet Union, her hometown—once known for being a major center of the automotive industry—experienced economic challenges. The transition away from a centrally planned economy, which is a characteristic of socialist systems like the Soviet Union, to a market economy brought fluctuations in employment and living standards, drastically impacting the local population.

"It's like time just stopped there," Dasha lamented. "My brother was older, and from what he told me, there [were] literally drugs in the street."

Dasha's parents weren't poor by Russian standards; her father worked as an engineer at the Volga Automotive Plant, and her mother was a lawyer. Nonetheless, they had to sell their home to fund Dasha's dreams.

"It's difficult when you are a twelve-year-old kid, and you realize that your parents are selling their dream in exchange for [yours]," she said. "[It's] difficult to accept that kind of pressure because you're not stupid, even if they don't say it to you. You can feel it."

In 2021, Dasha found a way to move through that pressure and began a comeback, reclaiming her place in the top ten. In team competition, Dasha played a crucial role in the 2020–21 Billie Jean King Cup, helping to secure Russia's first BJK Cup since 2008. In 2022, Dasha reached her highest ranking: #8 in the world and #1 in Russia.

That same year, Russia invaded Ukraine.

In response to the invasion, players representing Russia and Belarus were barred from competing at the 2022 Wimbledon Championships. The

International Olympic Committee ruled that Russians and Belarusians may participate in the Paris Games as neutral athletes without an accompanying flag, anthem, or country colors.

Dasha told the *New York Times* that she didn't mind being designated as neutral but was considering suggesting an alternative.

"I want to ask the [Women's Tennis Association] if I can play under the rainbow flag," Dasha said with a laugh.

In her interview with Vitya, Dasha's courage extended beyond her coming-out: She openly condemned the Russian invasion of Ukraine, calling it a "full-blown nightmare," despite such dissent being risky. It's likely she wouldn't have been allowed to represent Russia after her remarks anyway.

Since returning to the presidency in 2012, Vladimir Putin has been cracking down on the gay community and associated organizations. The intensified approach aligns with historical precedents, using "internal enemies" to drum up support for a government at war.

In Russia, Dasha faces the risk of fines and possible imprisonment for speaking out against the war and openly addressing her sexuality. Her high profile would make the authorities less likely to ignore her defiance. However, Dasha hasn't returned home since Russia attacked Ukraine in February of 2022.

"Living in the closet is impossible," Dasha declared. "Living in peace with yourself is the only thing that matters, and fuck everyone else."

As I write this, Dasha is ranked #11 in the world and lives in Spain with her girlfriend, the former Olympic figure skater Natalia Zabiiako.

As Dasha's interview with Vitya came to a close, she tearfully acknowledged that her stance against the war and her sexuality made returning home unlikely.

> "Living in the closet is impossible. Living in peace with yourself is the only thing that matters."

"Before the war started, I never appreciated the chance to go back. I always wanted to leave and live abroad. It's only when [the chance to go home is taken away] that you realize how much you need it," Dasha told the *Sunday Times*. "I want to be able to respect myself when I look in the mirror, and if being a good person means I have to sacrifice my home, that's my choice."

Dasha's decision to come out likely inspired countless individuals worldwide who face the same internal struggle. Motivated to come out by the bravery of Russian soccer player Nadya Karpova, who came out shortly before her, Dasha emphasized the importance of public figures speaking out.

"I believe it is important that influential people from sports, or any other sphere, really speak about it," Dasha told Vitya. "It is important for young people who have a hard time with society and need support."

Dasha has experienced a newfound sense of freedom that blunts the consequences, a heavy weight lifted from her shoulders. Her decision to be true to herself has come at a significant cost: She cannot return home. But it also showed her who was in her corner. The tennis community, among others, rallied around her, sending her messages of love and support.

"As a gay person who opposes the war, it's not possible to go back," she said in an interview with the *Sunday Times*. "But I don't regret it even one percent. When the war started and everything turned to hell, I felt very overwhelmed, and I just decided, 'Fuck it all.'

"I couldn't hide it anymore. I wanted to say my position on the war and my [sexuality], which was tough coming from a country where being gay is not accepted. Afterward, I faced a few consequences, but the only thing that worried me was my parents, and they were fine. They are proud of me," Dasha explained.

Dasha's family is a sticking point for her, and she gets emotional when the topic comes up. Two of her three brothers live in Canada, while one, Alexsandr, travels with her and serves as her fitness trainer. Dasha and her siblings had all hoped their parents would leave Russia, but they didn't want to start new lives in a new place. While Dasha's mom has visited her in Spain, she hasn't seen her father since 2021.

"It's hard not being able to see the people I love on a regular basis. In fact, I can barely see them," she said. "Even when this war finishes, we don't know how it's going to end up, particularly in Russia—if I will be able to go back or not."

It's a sacrifice Dasha was willing to make. Her visibility offers hope to a generation of LGBTQ+ Russians who yearn for the day when they can live authentically, proudly, and out. These days, Dasha and Natalia freely post about their sports and their lives on social media.

"All these parts are always behind the scenes," Dasha said. "Nobody knows about it: Ninety-five percent of the fans see us as tennis players on the tennis court. They don't know who we are outside of the court, how we live, or what's going on, actually, behind the tennis court doors."

It only takes a few minutes of watching her to see that Dasha is happy, caring, and comfortable in her skin. But the journey to self-acceptance is a complex and ongoing process.

As Dasha and I navigated the landscapes of our respective hometowns, we hope that others can do the same, lighting the way for those who seek to embrace their truth. And we hope, too, that in time our places of origin will open up, come to accept that there are so many ways to lead a life, learn to embrace those who are different. Whether deep in the heart of Texas or the vast expanse of Russia, we all want a home where we are accepted for who we are.

To Dasha, the Grand Slam Champion of "Fuck Everyone Else"— thank you.

"WHEN I THINK ABOUT STRENGTH, I THINK ABOUT BEING TRUE TO YOURSELF. I THINK YOU ARE YOUR STRONGEST WHEN YOU'RE BEING AUTHENTICALLY YOU."

Simone Manuel

They Fight the Patriarchy

THE REGGAE GIRLZ

By Chidinma Iwu

It was early summer 2023, and the upcoming Women's World Cup promised a month packed full of soccer goodness. What could be better?

A lot, as it turned out.

The first problem was the derisory prize money. Even though it was an increase from 2019, it was still so much less than what the winners of the most recent men's World Cup had received. The purse seemed like a deliberate and blatant communication of how little the world values women (as if we didn't already know).

The next issue was that many of the qualified teams were being grossly underpaid by their national soccer federations. Elite teams from all over the world, from Spain to Vietnam and beyond, had dealt with distasteful training camp and transportation conditions just to be in Australia and New Zealand for 2023.

All this was obscene, but not particularly surprising—which I guess shows just how low my expectations were for the governing bodies of women's soccer. But the detail I was completely unprepared to learn about, the part that sent me into a pure rage fit, was that Jamaica's team would have to crowdfund enough money to compete in the World Cup.

Left: Kameron Simmonds of Jamaica defends the ball

That's right. Jamaica's national women's soccer team had qualified for the World Cup for the second time in history. They had earned the opportunity to play on a stage that would hold the eyes of the world. Yet their government wouldn't fund their trip.

I couldn't work out what I felt more strongly: anger at the glaring discrimination or amazement at the talent and perseverance of these Caribbean women in the face of it.

The first time I saw Jamaica's Reggae Girlz fly in green, yellow, and specks of black—a color blend that reminded me of good music and long hair—their opponents were South Africa's Banyana Banyana in a 2019 friendly match. This was the first time I saw Khadija "Bunny" Shaw play, the phenomenal striker who would become captain of the Jamaican team.

Despite its name, the match's first half was tough, grueling, and not so friendly at all. The fieriness, zeal, and everything else that makes me love women's soccer was evident in both teams. But one of them was leading this fight, and it wasn't the Girlz. Shaw made a goal attempt in the seventeenth minute, but it was futile and the team's performance slacked afterward. Meanwhile Banyana Banyana dominated in ball possession and passes and goal attempts, a hot pursuit of victory that gave them a goal by the end of the first half.

When both teams came in for the second half of the game, though, the Girlz had gotten into their groove. Jamaica rallied quickly and scored an equalizing goal that I never saw coming, one that wiped the smug look off South Africa's face. Banyana Banyana were notably still ahead in overall game performance, but the Girlz had impressed me and thousands of other viewers. They had also denied their hosts their first win of the year. That was some shit.

Jamaica's potential was impossible to ignore. The odds were stacked against them, but they had built a team strong enough to qualify for that year's Women's World Cup for the first time ever. This achievement was despite—not because of—their governing body.

The Jamaica Football Federation (JFF)—a consortium of chauvinists—defunded their women's national team in 2008 to focus on their men's team (which had not qualified for any men's World Cup since 1998). When Cedella Marley, daughter of the legendary Bob Marley, prodded the federation for an explanation, they gave the flimsy excuse of having to prioritize due to a lack of sufficient funds. There were no reports of unseriousness from the women, nor was there any basis of merit from the men. Nonetheless, the JFF disbanded the women's team and invested all their resources into developing the men's. Almost as if the Reggae Boyz were the default, and the Girlz were a subgroup that had to wait in line for some powerful economic development to sweep the country before getting their chance.

The federation's response pissed off Marley—like it would any right-thinking person—and she took it upon herself to ensure that the Girlz could keep playing. With her brothers, Marley wrote songs about the Girlz and led online fundraisers to help cover the costs of their travel and games. Despite these efforts, the team didn't qualify for the 2015 Women's World Cup. But Marley and the Girlz pressed on, and in 2019, they became the first Caribbean team to qualify for the Women's World Cup.

You might expect that this milestone would have elicited some sort of consideration from the JFF—maybe some training sponsorships, or resource investment into their professional development. The women's team showed even more potential than the Boyz; they had made it to the world stage with no institutional support. Surely they had proven themselves.

Just kidding! There was still no government-backed support for the Girlz as they pushed through the first round of World Cup matches on reserve funds from their GoFundMe campaigns. They lost all their group stage matches and returned home, defeated and still on their own.

In 2023, these remarkable athletes woke up an umpteenth time, dusted off their boots, and again qualified for the World Cup. But how could the team possibly afford to go to Australia?

They launched another fundraiser. This time, midfielder Havana Solaun's mother joined Marley in amplifying the cause. Sandra Phillips-Brower, Solaun's mother, told the Special Broadcasting Service (SBS), "If I can somehow make this journey smoother for them, and let them focus on what they'd love to do—play soccer—they shouldn't be worried about the politics or getting a flight or getting accommodation."

Bunny Shaw posted a long, pain-filled statement on her Instagram page about the team's disappointment with the federation's disrespect for them. Citing the lack of resources and compensation—which made it needlessly difficult for them to prepare for the tournament—Shaw expressed a decade of pent-up frustration.

"We have also showed up repeatedly without receiving contractually agreed upon compensation," she wrote, adding that the JFF had promised to resolve the Girlz' concerns in a timely manner. "Unfortunately, that time has expired and once again our questions go unanswered and our concerns unresolved."

Shaw's post brought in nearly ten thousand likes and hundreds of comments in solidarity with the Girlz. The JFF put out a poor excuse of a public statement to clarify missing context, ending with a shameful appreciation of the public for donating to the Girlz' World Cup appearance.

Together—and no thanks to the JFF—Phillips-Brower, Marley, and the team raised the money they needed. The Girlz were going to Australia.

The second time I watched the Reggae Girlz fly, it was at the start of the 2023 Women's World Cup, on a hot summer morning. I was rooting for my own national team, the Super Falcons of Nigeria, to win the cup, but I swore not to miss any of Jamaica's matches. This time, the color blend of green, yellow, and black reminded me not only of excellent music but also of badass women with comebacks that could throw opponents off their feet. Man, was I *sat*?

They played against France's Les Bleues, a team that had won all ten of their World Cup qualifying matches as European heavyweights. When the two teams played in a 2014 friendly match, France had beaten Jamaica 8–0. This time, though, I saw the Girlz hold their own in a tough start, striking accurate passes despite the expertise of a determined France.

Rebecca Spencer owned her goalpost, Deneisha Blackwood lit fires with her domination of defense, Cheyna Matthews held the field in that center, and Shaw pushed France's buttons in a way their past ten opponents had not. This was a better team than I'd seen in 2019, and the fact that everyone could witness this improvement against a team like Les Bleues was a remarkable feat of its own. Jamaica came into the World Cup ranked forty-third in the FIFA Women's World Ranking, while France came in ranked fifth—yet on this field, they seemed evenly matched. The Girlz worked their way around France's control of the game and ensured that every goal attempt by Les Bleues was futile. This match was goalless and yet exceptional.

But near the end of the match, something happened that seemed like it could spell the end for the Girlz. Shaw, Jamaica's top scorer, fouled a French player and got a red card. She was sent out of the tournament.

Jamaica's performance in the next match seemed sure to waver without their star player on the pitch.

But did it? Hardly.

Jamaica's second World Cup game, six days later, was a sweet, clean victory against their Central American counterpart Panama. Watching them run around with coordination, clear heads, and accurate passing felt almost like a religious revival. The Girlz were valiant in the absence of their captain. When Allyson Swaby sent a shot flying into the goal, it felt unreal for the first few seconds—but *boy*, was it real. That was one of the *hardest* goals of the tournament. It shook the stadium and captured the hearts of soccer viewers around the world.

The first stage of an international soccer tournament, also called the group stage, is critical. Each team plays three matches, and the sixteen teams that finish those matches with the best records advance to the knockout rounds. There's no set number of wins that you must have. You just need to ensure you're not at the bottom.

The draw with Les Bleues meant one point for Jamaica. The win over Panama gave them another three. To advance to the next stage, Jamaica would need to achieve a win or a tie in their third match, against Brazil. So the Girlz amped up defense and prepared to battle.

Every goal attempt from the South Americans was met with a cohesive defense and Spencer's saves. The match was a goalless draw. Brazil, a traditional soccer powerhouse and South America's most successful national

What the Reggae Girlz showed us is that the patriarchy does not always win.

team, was out of the World Cup. The Girlz were in the round of sixteen—the first Caribbean team ever to make it that far.

It was torturous to know that such an extraordinary team had needed to crowdfund their trip to Australia. It was appalling that they received no institutional support to meet the teams they played and bested, to experience international recognition for the first time. The JFF offered all sorts of excuses, but this was really just a simple case of how the patriarchy *tries to* impede women's dreams everywhere. From places as small as the home to stages as big as the World Cup.

What the Reggae Girlz showed us is that the patriarchy does not always win. For as strong as these male-dominated systems are, the will of women is stronger.

The fifth time I watched the Reggae Girlz fly, it was August 8, 2023, in the round of sixteen. My heart swelled as I watched green, yellow, and black race across the field in swift attacks and a nearly impenetrable defense against Colombia. *They were here.* It was a historic, nearly impossible feat that would cement the team's status as champions whether they won or not—and whether the JFF liked it or not.

"*WHENEVER PEOPLE SAY 'WOMEN'S SOCCER,' I WANT TO CORRECT THEM TO SAY 'SOCCER.'*"

Alex Morgan

They Trust Their Bodies

SMASHING A TABOO IN WOMEN'S SPORTS

By Aileen Weintraub

It was a beautiful spring day in Ibiza, Spain, where the backdrop of sun, sea, and sand was the perfect setting for the 2023 PTO European Open. Highly decorated thirty-six-year-old British triathlete Emma Pallant-Browne, known as one of the best multisport athletes in the world, was running in a light-colored pink bathing suit. She was making great time when the unexpected happened. She got her period.

Pallant-Browne did what any professional athlete would do: She kept running. She had a finish line to cross. There was no way she was going to start looking for someone on the sidelines to spot her a tampon.

Instead of revering Pallant-Browne for her perseverance, keyboard warriors around the world judged the photo of her running in her blood-stained bathing suit, which was posted online after the event. Some commenters suggested that the photo was in poor taste and should be cropped.

Pallant-Browne could have ignored these comments or insisted the photo be taken down, but instead she doubled down, posting the photo to her own Instagram page with a message championing women in sports and the barriers they face, including the unglamorous reality of sometimes competing while bleeding:

Left: Heather Watson

If you wrote to me saying 99% of the women you know would be mortified at this, then that is exactly why I am sharing this, because there really is nothing wrong. It's natural. . . . So if you have a photo like this, save it, cherish it, remember how you performed on a tough day, because one day you might just be able to help someone else.

Men and women began stepping up to support Pallant-Browne, and her photo went viral, with comments focusing on her skill and strength as an athlete. This was no small moment in the fight for women's equality in sports. Up to 25 percent of elite female athletes don't have regular menstrual cycles, usually due to overtraining and underfueling of food and hydration. Pallant-Browne was telling the world that an athlete who gets their period should be celebrated—or, at the very least, treated with respect rather than disgust.

Shame and criticism are only some of the difficulties of being a menstruating athlete. During that time of the month, training and play time can be affected, challenging performance, contributing to exhaustion, and adding to mental stress. A 2021 study of elite female soccer players in the journal *Science and Medicine in Football* found that 93 percent felt a reduction in power and 87 percent felt increased fatigue when menstruating, while more than 66 percent found their focus negatively impacted. When an athlete is competing for a championship, no matter the level, these issues can be a major setback.

With women already fighting for equality on the pitch, the lack of support and the stigma around menstruation often discourage players from participating and can be a blow to their confidence. Luckily, female athletes around the world, both in professional and amateur sports, are advocating for change.

The US women's soccer team confronted these obstacles head-on in 2019, fully prepared to make sure that the team's menstrual cycles didn't get in the way of taking home the Women's World Cup. They collectively tracked their periods to help them decide what to eat, how much to hydrate, and how to structure their workouts. They even had posters throughout their lodging to remind them of the different phases of their cycle and how to treat their bodies. It paid off. Dealing with their periods openly, refusing to feel ashamed of their strong bodies, and getting their coaches involved helped ensure their historic win.

While periods have always been a concern for elite athletes playing at the highest levels, the issue affects young competitors as well. According to research funded by menstrual product manufacturer Always, nearly one out of every two girls will drop out of sports during puberty, often because they have low body confidence or are embarrassed by their period. Additionally, a Women in Sport study found that seven out of every ten girls will refrain from participating in sports during their periods. This is in part because many young athletes don't feel comfortable discussing their menstrual cycle with their coaches.

Of the fourteen thousand athletes surveyed for the adidas Watch Us Move campaign, including those at the top of their profession, 82 percent of athletes in the United Kingdom said they never learned about the correlation between sports and their menstrual cycle, and of those who had a coach, 82 percent confessed they had never spoken to them about their period. These numbers are only slightly better in the United States, with 65 percent of athletes saying they were never educated about how menstruation can affect athletic abilities and 76 percent admitting they never discussed their cycle with their coach. Unfortunately, studies show that both male and female coaches feel they don't have enough information to adequately support their players.

Another obstacle is that talking about periods means talking about reproductive health, which is associated with . . . you guessed it. SEX. Coaches are concerned about crossing the line. In a 2023 POPSUGAR article, author Christine Yu of *Up to Speed: The Groundbreaking Science of Women Athletes* said, "This makes it more difficult for coaches to talk to girls about, because it seems inappropriate." Given the potential for sex scandals, coaches have good reason to be concerned. The problem is, if players don't feel safe discussing these issues with their coaches, then they can't benefit from their coaches' guidance either.

Unsurprisingly, period stigma around female athletes dates all the way back to ancient Greek and Roman societies, which perpetuated the myth

"You can uphold tradition and still move with the times."

that strenuous physical activity would affect a woman's reproductive abilities. This harmful falsehood lasted well into the twentieth century. As late as the 1970s, the Amateur Athletic Union (AAU), the organization that governs amateur competitive sports in the United States, forbade women from competing in races longer than 1.5 miles. Two long-distance runners, Nina Kuscsik and Kathrine Switzer—who were both told by medical professionals that running would make it difficult for them to conceive and that their uteruses might fall out—decided it was time to change this antiquated rule. Their hard work was well rewarded. In 1971, the AAU changed the regulation. In 1972, Kuscsik became the official first women's winner of the New York City Marathon, and in 1974, Switzer took the title. Not a single uterus fell out.

The battle to make the sports world more accessible to menstruating athletes is ongoing. In 2022, tennis player Gabriella Holmes and soccer player Holly Gordon organized the Address the Dress Code campaign outside Wimbledon. Women protested the tournament's all-white dress code by wearing red shorts under white skirts and holding up signs that read, "About bloody time." Who doesn't have traumatic memories of wearing all white and suddenly realizing it's that time of the month? Now imagine having to worry about this happening while being televised in front of an audience of millions.

The last thing pro athletes need at a major competition is one more thing to worry about. "You can uphold tradition and still move with the times," Holmes said during a 2022 interview with the *Guardian*, explaining that the goal of the protest was to relieve stress and shame while competing on the world stage.

Another player who has taken up the cause is British tennis pro Heather Watson, who said that she began using birth control just to avoid leakage and embarrassment. Back in 2015, she gave a post-match interview to the BBC after disappointing at the Australian Open, confessing that she felt lightheaded and low on energy because of "girl things."

With the heat turned up, Wimbledon finally addressed period concerns in 2023, officially allowing women to wear dark undershorts beneath their white outfits during competitions. This may have been one small, significant step for tennis players, but it was a giant leap for the menstruating masses.

More and more sports are ditching the white shorts and replacing them with rag-friendly attire. The Orlando Pride is the first National Women's Soccer League team to change their uniforms based solely on period concerns. Manchester City Women, along with other English teams, also announced that players would no longer be wearing white shorts during games, and in 2023, the Irish women's rugby team swapped their traditional white duds for navy.

Of course, period problems go way beyond attire. Tennis player Zheng Qinwen from China was killing it in the opener against her opponent Iga Świątek of Poland during the 2022 French Open, but she was forced to take a medical time-out in the next round. She could be seen having her back massaged on court and struggled through the rest of the sets with intense stomach pain. During an interview with CNN, she later explained it was the first day of her period, which is always the toughest for her, lamenting, "I wish I can be a man on court . . . [so] that I don't have to suffer from this." Zheng didn't owe anyone an explanation, but in speaking frankly about the cause of her discomfort, she reminded everyone that periods don't need to be kept secret.

Another Chinese athlete, swimmer Fu Yuanhui, went viral for discussing how her period affected her swim time in a post-race interview during the 2016 Olympics. Fu's team had just barely missed winning a medal in the 4 x 100-meter medley relay. As her teammates were interviewed, she was crouching in pain. When it was her turn to speak, she stood up, clearly struggling and being physically supported by her teammates while she held on to the railing. Instead of brushing off the interviewer's suggestion that she had a stomachache, she told the world what it's like for an athlete to compete at an Olympic level while bleeding, saying, "It's because I just got my period yesterday, so I'm still a bit weak and really tired." The result was a social media firestorm that educated viewers about swimming while menstruating and praised Fu for boldly speaking out. In China, where television commercials advertising feminine hygiene products are banned during prime time, her candidness was a huge win.

Inspired by Fu, Japanese swimmer and two-time Olympian Hanae Ito has made it her mission to open up the conversation of menstruation for Japanese athletes. In 2017, she spoke out about how having her period during the 2008 Olympics affected her timing, and she wished she had been made aware of available options to help with period-related weight gain. It was only once she retired that she finally saw a female physician who addressed her symptoms.

Hanae has since founded the 1252 Project, named for the twelve weeks out of a year that most women are forced to deal with their periods. The project educates the public about the challenges female athletes have when it comes to their cycle. She is facing off against the unwritten code that women aren't supposed to mention the bloat, cravings, nausea, headaches, lower back pain, and cramps.

In India, where discussing menstruation is taboo and only 29 percent of women participate in sports, it's only recently that athletes have opened up about their periods. During an interview with *Sportstar,* Indian javelin thrower Annu Rani explained how she overcame cramps and set a national record at the World Athletics Championships. It was an Olympic qualifying event, and she had no choice but to push through the pain. She wasn't allowed to take pain meds and the cramping brought her to tears. So many women can relate.

Rani confessed that it took her a long time to feel confident enough to train during her period, and she emphasized the importance of connecting with senior athletes for support and advice. "Many people call menstruation dirty. I don't understand what's so dirty about it when the process helps us in giving birth. I urge people to understand the science behind it, ditch the myths, and listen to their bodies."

Luckily, in India, change is being implemented on a large scale. The women's hockey team now keeps track of their cycles on period tracker apps, and Olympic Gold Quest, an organization established to support India's athletes, works with nutritionists to help players manage cramps, exhaustion, and other symptoms. Since iron deficiency is common among Indian women, in part due to their vegetarian lifestyle, athletes are also screened for anemia, and any period-related issues are addressed well in advance of competitions. Change like this can only be effective after a certain level of trust has been built by consenting adults, and with a clear understanding that tracking will be used for specific purposes: to help the athlete train appropriately during each phase of their cycle, not to discriminate against or shame them.

Despite the success of awareness campaigns, some male athletes have demonstrated how much work is left to be done. Famed golfer Tiger Woods went viral in 2023 for all the wrong reasons when he not-sodiscreetly placed a tampon in competitor Justin Thomas's hand during the Genesis Invitational. The tampon was supposed to convey that Thomas played like a girl, but instead, it further highlighted that male athletes like Woods have no clue how much focus, concentration, and pure grit it takes to compete while bleeding. If the world's top male athletes bled for a total of three months a year, it's safe to assume that endless funding, documentaries, and trophies would be handed out just for showing up. Woods later apologized for his misogyny, spurring discussions on social media and in the press about period poverty and other obstacles women face when it comes to menstruation.

While Woods may be living back in the Stone Age, other pro athletes around the world are using their platforms to stand up to discrimination, and the momentum to smash old stereotypes is only growing. In 2022, fifty elite athletes joined together for the #SayPeriod campaign, believing that change begins when we get comfortable saying the word out loud. Many more are tossing their pads and 'pons for menstrual cups—which can be used for longer amounts of time while also cutting down on the chance of leakage—and using apps not only to track their periods but also to keep tabs on their energy levels and nutritional needs during their cycle.

Destigmatizing this historically taboo topic by normalizing bleeding and embracing menstruation helps level the playing field. When the top echelon of women's sports emphasizes period awareness, it has a trickle-down effect, signaling to young players that there's no place for shame or secrecy. Nearly half the people in the world get their period, and that includes elite athletes. The days of hiding it are over.

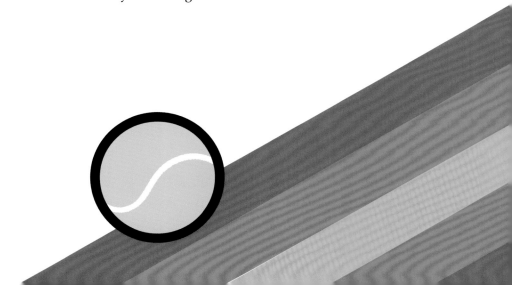

FAILURE IS NOT AN OPTION FOR JENNY HOFFMAN

By Tonya Russell

Jenny Hoffman is a Harvard physicist. She's published her research in journals with names like *Journal of Electron Spectroscopy and Related Phenomena*, and her faculty bio includes the phrases "quasiparticle interference" and "nanoscale electronic phase transitions." I do not, to be totally honest, have any idea what Jenny does.

But understanding the fickle behavior of subatomic particles is only part of what differentiates Jenny from most of us. The other part is that she's an ultramarathoner. In 2019, Jenny set out to cross the United States on foot. She trained and prepared for months.

Even the idea of driving 3,000 miles sounds exhausting to many, but ever since she was a child, Jenny had "always dreamed about crossing the US under [her] own power," she said. Descriptions of the country's diverse landscapes in "America the Beautiful" filled her with wonder, and she was curious about the various subcultures she'd heard about. The country offered so much to smell, see, and taste, and little Jenny wanted to experience it all.

According to Jenny, "I think there's something really glorious about seeing all of that at a pace that you can control." As a child, she romanticized crossing the country by bike. But when she finally embarked upon this journey at the age of forty, it would look quite different than she'd envisioned, and she'd swap her bike for multiple pairs of HOKA shoes. She set her mind on running from San Francisco to New York City. She wanted the interactions that this slower speed would allow.

Despite the logistics and physical challenges that awaited her, Jenny was confident. After all, running was her favorite pastime. Her profession, being a physicist and a professor who managed a research group, was taxing. Being on the road requires far less thinking. "A lot of what I do is decision-making," she explained. "While I enjoy detailed problem-solving, the managerial aspect is something I find really stressful. When I'm running, I don't have to make any decisions."

All Jenny needed to do was put one foot in front of the other, and even though it would be a painful and long endeavor, there were few decisions involved. "It's like a brain break from my day-to-day job, and I am grateful to have an opportunity for a brain break."

With her mind made up and her body trained, Jenny hit the road in 2019.

She did not reach New York. Her attempt at the world record—being the fastest woman to run across the United States—ended six days from when she was slated to finish. She said, "I made it 2,560 miles and blew out my knee in Akron, Ohio."

Needless to say, Jenny was heartbroken. She had been running at well under record pace, and going home to rehab her torn meniscus would be an arduous process. But her dream was still there. She prepared her mind and body to try again.

Her next attempt was in 2022, but this time Jenny wouldn't even make it to the starting line. Jenny tore her hamstring right before she was set to begin, and she was forced to trade a cross-country trek for pool rehab and physical therapy. Through her platelet-rich plasma injections and down-time, she was determined to get back out there.

When she'd regained her fitness, Jenny was ready to attempt another run from San Francisco to New York City. She left San Francisco City Hall on September 16, 2023, and like her first journey, she was accompanied by friends: five women who took turns running with her, offering moral support and keeping her company. They also managed her food stops and carried her sunscreen. When they weren't running, they retired to the RV that trailed behind them for six hours of sleep.

The unfinished attempt in 2019 made some parts of the journey feel familiar, and with that came feelings of trepidation. With an idea of what was to come, and getting mentally prepared to run daily for over a month, Jenny attempted to journal on her Strava along the way. "I was determined to capture this experience in words," she explained.

Early on, Jenny gained 7 pounds from edema, which was caused by the high-mileage running, and she had to run through shin splints that nearly derailed her plans. Despite being an advanced runner, Jenny struggled. In the sixth day of her journal entries, she lamented early on about the challenges:

> Today was a rough start and a strong finish, but I couldn't have done it without the terrific support of my team.
>
> Nevada was the toughest state for me in 2019—then I suffered through 8 days of excruciating shin splints and had to take 1.5 days totally off moping in the RV. This year I was so determined to avoid the shin splints, and I thought I was being so much smarter—I started with lower mileage, better sleep and nutrition (protein smoothies for lunch and no Oreos allowed before I hit 50 miles!), and a slower descent from Tioga Pass (in 2019 I flew down so quickly I peed in my pants!).
>
> So yesterday afternoon I was feeling smug and relieved as I approached the Nevada border with shins feeling good . . . but in the final descent into Benton, the last town in California, the shin splints onset again suddenly and ferociously. Miscommunication about how much ibuprofen we had on hand (only six pills) and misunderstanding of the massage-gun power (does not work when battery is discharged, even when plugged in) sent me into a state of high anxiety, and I lay awake in bed until way too late. I woke up this morning with a cough and runny nose, and discovered that the Garmin watch had discharged overnight while "updating Amazon Music" and it was just too much. I set what felt like an impossible goal of 50 miles for the day and headed out the RV door in tears, an hour later than usual.
>
> At one point this afternoon a kind old gentleman passed me and turned around to pull over beside me. He asked, "Where are you headed?" I said "Boston." He stared at me blankly for a second then his face fell. He said, "I'm sorry, I was going to offer you a ride, but that's too far."

This is a long post because it will likely be several more days before we have service again, as we traverse the upcoming 169-mile, empty, treeless, and townless desert between Tonopah and Ely.

Outside of mental battles, Jenny faced external conflicts as well. The heat was relentless across the deserts of Utah and Nevada, and in Nebraska, Jenny battled headwinds and harvesting tractors that encroached on her shoulder space. Dogs and coyotes introduced themselves at various points across the country. On some days, she could look forward to reuniting with family, and on others, she relied on the promise of Pop-Tarts to get her to her stopping point. "There's lots of weather, and lots of animals," she recalled.

Through the trying times, the route still provided Jenny a look at the nation's beauty. She recalled one morning: "I was climbing in the dark under a clear sky, and just as I crested the pass, I watched as the moon was setting behind me and the sun was rising in front of me." That left a brilliant pink light and gold foliage before her. Nature was showing off for her.

There were also plenty of reminders of how kind people could be. The conversations with strangers carried her, and their gifts (such as fresh eggs) helped her along her journey. Crossing the country at 5 miles per hour can enable someone to see the United States in greater detail.

Jenny credits her crew, who became like sisters, for helping her along the way. She didn't have to carry much—nothing but a protein bar in her

Jenny Hoffman

pocket and Squirrel's Nut Butter to prevent chafing. She said, "I was very reliant on my team, who was leapfrogging me every few miles and providing what I needed along the way so I could run light."

Her team helped her run her daily average of 60 miles. While Jenny missed her church and her three children, her crew kept her spirited and focused on the goal.

No need to guess the best part of the trip: It was arriving in Manhattan and laying eyes on the skyline. The last 12-mile stretch was glorious and wiped away the struggles that preceded that day. Jenny's loved ones met her at the George Washington Bridge and ran her in to her finish.

Jenny surpassed the world record by an astonishing 7 days. It took her 47 days, 12 hours, and 35 minutes to reach her final destination. (The previous record, set in 2017 by Sandra Villines, was 54 days, 16 hours, and 24 minutes.) While she only needed 2,790 miles to break the record, Jenny finished with over 3,000 behind her.

Jenny has no plans to best her own record, but she still runs daily to give herself that "brain break." She sometimes replays days of her trip, thinking about how she could shave off time or tackle a patch of terrain differently, but there's not much she would change. She recalled, "Asking the body to hold up for that long [is] a risk. You could get hit by a car, you could run into a mountain lion, right? There's lots of things that can go wrong, and I feel really lucky that I was able to string together forty-eight days without anything going majorly wrong."

Jenny hopes that her run inspires others to explore the country. "I wish that everybody had an opportunity to move at pedestrian pace through so many communities and get to really see the humanity present within different lifestyles or backgrounds," she said.

It took three attempts and forty-five years for Jenny's childhood dream to be realized. There were times when she didn't make it—but there was one time when she did, and that's what sticks with her. As she said, "If you keep working, that failure won't be the end of your story."

They Row Together

RECOVERY ON WATER

By Allison Torres Burtka

Rowing is an intricate, choreographed dance with the water. You have to move the oars just right, and in unison, to use them as levers to propel you and your boat through the water. It's rhythmic and elegant.

But rowing is also tough: It requires upper- and lower-body strength, and it takes time to master the mechanics—a newbie can't just hop in a boat and expect it to go well.

Because rowing is physically demanding, it might seem like a bad idea for women who have been diagnosed with breast cancer, who may have physical limitations from treatment and may feel uneasy about what they and their bodies can do.

But, fortunately for the hundreds of women who have rowed with Recovery on Water (ROW), cofounders Sue Ann Glaser and Jenn Gibbons understood what rowing could offer to these women: a chance to reclaim their bodies and take charge of their own health.

Sue Ann was diagnosed with breast cancer in 2007, and her doctor said exercise would help mitigate the side effects of treatment and prevent a recurrence. But, she says, "I had been an exercise dropout for many, many years." Part of the reason was previous health issues that had limited the aerobic exercise she could do, but the other part was: "I hated exercise. I just hated it. I never found anything I liked."

At this point, though, Sue Ann knew she had to do something. "One of the great motivators was that my daughter was the same age that I had been when my mom died of breast cancer. So I wanted to do everything I could so that she wouldn't have to go through what I went through," she says. She'd heard about a rowing program in Boston for breast cancer survivors, and even though she'd never rowed, it seemed like something she could stick to. She looked for a program near her in the Chicago area, but it didn't exist. She thought about starting one.

It turns out another woman was trying to do the same thing, but coming at it as a coach: Jenn, who had rowed in college and had coached a program in Michigan for breast cancer survivors. They connected, and the duo, with Sue Ann in her sixties and Jenn in her twenties, founded ROW in 2007. They borrowed equipment from a high school and had their first practice in 2008 in Skokie, Illinois.

The women who showed up didn't quite know what they were getting into. But ROW gave them a way to keep exercising consistently and to be around women who understood what they were going through.

"It's not just any old rowing team—it's a rowing team for people whose existence has been threatened with cancer, whose control over their bodies has been smashed, who feel helpless, because this just happened to them out of the blue," Sue Ann says. "Rowing can be an antidote to all those things. You end up feeling so powerful and so good about your body as it grows and strengthens and learns new things."

Why rowing? Because it's tough. Because it forces you to be a team. Because it can be an adrenaline rush—but also calming and meditative. Even just being near the water can boost mental health, research has found.

Although rowing is rigorous full-body exercise, it's also low impact, so "it's accessible to a wide range of ages and body types," says Tara Hoffmann, executive director of ROW. "But it's also really fun. Rowing is the dream and not the drudgery that exercise can be."

Once you push the boat off the dock, "It's quiet. There's some sort of thing that comes over us—it becomes extremely peaceful somehow," says Mary Ridley, who joined ROW in 2015. Then when you settle in and start rowing, it's "the whole idea of swaying, the whole idea of moving together, feeling the boat move under us. It's just the most incredible thing."

The boat is moving backward, so you can't see where you're going—you have to trust your coxswain to steer. To get the timing right, you have to pay attention to the person in front of you and follow their movements. You hear the chunk sound of your oars turning in their oar locks and then your blades slipping into the water.

"It was in a way like flying," Sue Ann says. "Our minds were just in the boat, and just on the head or the person in front of us and following them and not paying any attention to anything else." For Sue Ann, this meant her nagging joint pain would just go away when she was on the water.

The team rows on the Chicago River six months out of the year and does indoor training on rowing machines, or "ergs," the rest of the year. They also run a summer camp in northern Michigan. ROW is part of the Survivor Rowing Network, which includes more than twenty cancer survivor rowing programs.

Many of the women who joined ROW didn't know how empowering sports could be, or they had never felt it themselves—ROW provided the path for them to become athletes.

"We poll our members when they join the team, and most of them do not identify as athletes," Tara says. "But then after a year on the team, nearly 90 percent of survey respondents said yeah, now I identify as an athlete."

That's what happened with Sue Ann. "Jenn talked to us from the very beginning about rowing in a regatta, which seemed ridiculous," she says. "At first, we said, you're nuts. And then she said, no, no, we can do this."

Sue Ann remembers racing for the first time: "We were way behind everybody else, but we finished the race. . . . We rowed our hearts out—there were cowbells and people yelling for us." On her way home from the regatta, Sue Ann had to stop at the supermarket. She got out of the car, wearing her spandex shorts and team T-shirt, and it hit her: "I found myself strutting across the parking lot, saying to myself, I am an athlete."

Tara first came to ROW in 2016, when she was forty-four, after being diagnosed with breast cancer. She remembers rowing at a regatta her first year, and the women in her boat had no idea how they would do against their competitors, who included college teams. But they won medals. "It is a new experience for a lot of our team members," she says.

That kind of experience proves you're really an athlete. "If someone hands you a medal, or if you see numbers on the performance monitor, and your coaches say, look at that improvement, look at what you can do—that's what really convinces people that they've stepped over a line and now they're a new person," Tara says.

ROW members range in age from thirty to eighty, and their experience with breast cancer and treatment varies.

"It's all ages, stages, and faces of cancer," Tara says. "We have women on the team diagnosed at stage zero all the way to stage four, or metastatic cancer. Those stage four athletes will always be in treatment."

Tara explains, "They're our baddest badasses, rowing through active treatment and cancer that is progressing. These are smart, committed athletes; they communicate to coaches what they can do and when they need to pull back. And it's a mixed bag, right? Sometimes the rowing can continue pretty easily for some time, and sometimes it just gets harder and harder and eventually has to stop. But it's very important to ROW that we are able to serve our stage four metastatic athletes with meaningful movement and a team for life."

The many side effects of breast cancer treatment can include diminished range of motion, swelling in the arms from lymph nodes being removed, and joint pain. The prevailing wisdom in the medical community used to be that breast cancer survivors should avoid exercise and not lift more than 5 to 10 pounds, but those recommendations have shifted to encourage exercise. And studies have shown that exercise can prevent recurrence—as much as a 55 percent lower risk of recurrence, one study found.

Choosing to row is "taking an active role in increasing our lifespan," Sue Ann says. She has now stopped rowing because of back problems—but only after rowing for thirteen years. "I loved every minute of it," she says. "I would have rowed till I'm one hundred if I could."

"I would have rowed till I'm one hundred if I could."

Tara had rowed in college but had been away from the sport for years. She joined when she was navigating treatment. "I was just getting really frustrated with being a passive patient, where there was not much that

Sue Ann Glaser and her crew

I could do. And my physical therapist, God bless him, asked if I had ever rowed before," she says. He was on ROW's board.

Tara jumped at the chance. "I wanted to get active. I wanted to challenge myself," she says. "But very quickly, the reason that I stayed was the friendships and the emotional support that I was getting, which I didn't really even realize that I needed."

"It's not a support group, where everyone's gonna come together and expect to share about themselves and what's hard," Tara says. "But there are a lot of small moments during practice where cancer things can be shared, or just an understanding of a shared experience."

Sue Ann adds, "We don't have to talk about breast cancer with anybody there. But if we want to or need to, everybody around us knows what we're going through."

Tara later started coaching for ROW, then joined the staff, and stepped in as executive director in 2022.

With some of the newcomers, Tara says, "You can see in their eyes that they are a little bit like deer in the headlights. They don't yet feel comfortable in their bodies coming out of cancer treatment, and there's a lot to learn in this strange new sport."

But then they feel the physical and mental benefits of rowing, plus the camaraderie. ROW surveys have shown that the team improves quality of life. Ninety-five percent of members said they feel like part of a community and less alone.

Tara Hoffmann and her crew

Tara remembers one woman who joined just a day or two before her mastectomy. "She begged me to get on the water," Tara says. "She knew that she wasn't gonna be able to continue with the team until she had healed. She was like, 'I've just got to know that this is here for me when I get back.'"

Mary, now seventy-eight, joined after being diagnosed but before she'd had any treatment. A friend brought her to an open house. "What I appreciated most was that the women who were there were from these different years of diagnosis, and it was kind of hopeful, having just been diagnosed and not gone through anything that all these women had gone through already," she says. "It was very reassuring."

When she joined, Mary was an active person—going to the gym, doing yoga, and cycling—but she never played sports in high school or college. "I had no real concept of what a rowing team would be like," she says.

Now she's been at it for more than nine years. "The rowing part of it can be very hard, can be very frustrating," Mary says. "You feel like 'I can't, I can't,' and we always do. And that I think is what is amazing about it, because we always say it's so, so hard, but we keep on going."

Power is an essential element in rowing, and rowing will show you your power. You can feel it as the boat moves, and you can see it. When your oar slips out of the water after pushing the boat along, a deep swirl of water takes its place, evidence that you've made something happen.

The team includes people from many different backgrounds, experiences, and personalities. Mary says, "I think I've said on more than one occasion, 'I don't think I would be your friend unless we were on this team. I would never have met someone like you, you crazy thing.'"

ROW has grown to more than ninety women on the current team roster, including twenty-two novices. Now, Tara aims to "focus our outreach in Chicago's historically underserved neighborhoods, underserved both in cancer treatment and in those posttreatment services," which would make the team more diverse racially and socioeconomically, she says. "Cancer doesn't discriminate, and ROW strives to fully represent Chicago area breast cancer survivors."

Mary calls herself one of the team's elders. She and another rower in her seventies say, "Well, when we turn eighty, maybe we'll cut ourselves some slack—you know, not try so hard," she says. "But I doubt that that will happen. Because I'm not as competitive as some of the women on the team, but man, I don't know, you put a few of us together and everybody wants to finish well."

Mary loves seeing women become rowers. "As awful as it is to meet the requirement for being on our particular team, as breast cancer survivors, it is just great to see how many novices, new members, we have who get totally hooked," she says.

These women go from "feeling really pretty shitty about life" to gaining confidence and taking charge, Mary says. She explains: "This is something I have chosen. I didn't choose any of this other stuff that happened to me, but I have chosen to learn this really tough thing. I've chosen to be here on a Sunday at eight in the morning and be ready to go and do some hard things."

Mary says, "That is a really powerful thing, I think, for each person to feel that they have agency."

Mary Ridley

They Decide What to Wear

BREAKING THROUGH DRESS CODES IN SPORTS

By Shireen Ahmed

I remember falling in love with soccer at the age of five and feeling like the world finally understood me. I was quick-thinking and fast, and I had a good game IQ. I was not the strongest player, but I worked hard at my skills. And it gave me a sense of belonging. The ball did not discriminate— unlike many people at the predominantly white school in the very white city where I grew up as a young Brown girl.

I passed this love of sports on to my children, two of whom play on university teams in Canada. My daughter turned out to be more skilled on the field than I ever was; she now represents Pakistan in soccer at the international level.

My daughter and I both wear a hijab, a religious headscarf. I chose to start at twenty, and she chose to start at fifteen. This made us outliers in competitive sports, where uniforms are the norm and deviation from that uniform look—like wearing a hijab—attracts attention.

The reasons for wearing a hijab are many. Mine is that I believe God commanded me to dress and behave modestly. That doesn't mean I can't be an athlete, an active wife and mom, a journalist, or a professor. I am all those things, and I wear a hijab. It's a way for me to embrace my faith, to be physically wrapped in a form of worship. It's my choice, and that makes me feel liberated and happy.

"Sports is a part of my identity, but so is my faith."

I spoke with my twenty-two-year-old daughter, Rumaysa, about her choice to wear a hijab as an athlete. "Sports is a part of my identity, but so is my faith," she said over one of our regular WhatsApp video calls. "I didn't see girls who wore a hijab around me when I played soccer or basketball at club level, or professionally or on television. But now there are players like Nouhaila Benzina [the Moroccan professional soccer player], and I love it." I asked Rumaysa if she ever felt like her hijab would prevent her from advancing in sports. "I never thought it was or could be a barrier."

Over the years, not everyone in the sports world has understood my daughter's choice to wear a hijab. Growing up, many of her coaches and teammates had few other Muslim friends. And so we taught people as we went along. Rumaysa is possibly the only hijab-wearing player in all of Canada Women's Soccer programs. She is by no means the only Muslim player, though. Not all Muslim women decide to cover. Choice is imperative, and we are taught this in Islam.

Unfortunately, the issue of covering is often thought of by outsiders as an imposition rather than a woman's choice. In plenty of cases, that is also true. In some countries like Iran, women do not have the right to choose how to dress on the court, on the pitch, or even in society. In Saudi Arabia, Muslim women playing sports are required to wear leggings underneath their gym shorts. Their attire is mandated by the government, taking away their bodily agency.

While there are places where female athletes are required to be covered, there are other instances where female athletes are not *allowed* to be covered. These situations might sound like opposites, but really, they're two sides of the same coin.

I have written about hijab bans and the exclusion of Muslim women in sports for over twelve years, and I know that any type of uniform restriction or dress code is a way to control women's bodies and deny them agency. I have said it many times: Forcing women out of clothing is as violent as forcing them into it.

FIFA, the world-governing body for soccer, and FIBA, the world-governing body for basketball, were both organizations that, until quite recently, forbade players from wearing hijabs. This rule was ostensibly for player-safety reasons but more likely thanks to racism. Maintaining this policy cost these sports some of their best players—not to mention countless girls and women who were being told, not in so many words, that they didn't belong on the field or the court.

One such player was Bilqis Abdul-Qaadir, who set the all-time scoring record in Massachusetts during her high school basketball career. After a successful showing in the NCAA, she hoped to go pro. But because of the ban on head coverings, she was forced—like so many other women—to make a choice between faith and sports.

After years of campaigning by Bilqis and other athletes in similar situations, FIFA changed its headscarf policy in 2014, and FIBA followed in 2017. Women are now free to practice their faith while pursuing their athletic ambitions.

These rulings should apply everywhere. But in France, the fight is ongoing.

France's policy of laïcité (secularism) means that any religious object—including a hijab—is considered a danger to French culture and society. Secularism insists that social and public society should not be subjected to religious objects or symbolism.

Hélène Bâ is a twenty-two-year-old graduate student in France studying criminology and humanitarian law, and she is the cofounder of Basket pour Toutes, a collective advocating for women's freedom to cover as they like while competing in sports.

Hélène started playing basketball at five years old. She played on a team exclusively with boys, some of whom did not think she belonged on the court. "I think it's at that moment I discovered sexism," she told me. "So believe me when I say that my first battles for equality took place on the court, fighting (by playing) to prove I deserve my sport."

Hélène's father is from Senegal, and her mother is a white Muslim from France. She identifies as being a *baller*—but because she lives in a country that insists on keeping her away from basketball so long as she observes her religion, that relationship is fragmented.

"Basketball is a passion to me," Hélène wrote. "I never wanted to go pro or be the best player in the world. I love the hardship of practice and

Hélène Bâ

the sacrifices you make for your team. Seventeen years later I still love this sport so much, but it's become intertwined with a lot of bad memories, struggles, and activism. I just want to be on the court with my teammates (who all became my friends) during competitions, laugh with them at practice, and end up running laps with them when our coach is mad."

Hélène doesn't want to quit basketball, but, she said, "I may end up choosing another sport to play in a championship that does not have such a ban."

Some French Muslim athletes do find themselves in a position where they must quit their sports. Others quit the country. Soccer player Lina Boussaha, for example, left the famous club Paris Saint-Germain when, in her early twenties, she started wearing a hijab. She was able to continue her career when she was offered a spot on the roster for Saudi Arabia's Al Nassr.

In July 2021, we saw another case of women not being granted choice over what to wear while playing sports. At the European Beach Handball Championships, the Norwegian team—tired of being sexualized for their bodies rather than respected for their accomplishments—wore shorts over their mandated bikinis as a sign of protest. For this alleged violation of covering their bottoms, they were fined 150 euros per player by the International Handball Federation (IHF). An entire global campaign started via social media, and the pop superstar P!nk even offered to pay their fees. Within months, the IHF had changed the rules, now allowing female athletes to wear shorts more similar to their male counterparts.

I'm glad that the Norwegian team's protest worked, and I would like to see the world rally around Muslim women in the same way. We often witness a type of selective feminism that will defend Norwegian handball players but not Black or Brown Muslim women, who have historically been weighed down by gendered Islamophobia and people making decisions for them about how they dress.

Ironically, in the same month that the Norwegian team was fined for wearing clothes that covered too much, Welsh Paralympian Olivia Breen was criticized for wearing clothes that were too revealing. She shared on social media that an official at the English Championships had told her that the bottoms in her long jump outfit were "too short and inappropriate."

In 2011, the Badminton World Federation tried to require elite female players to wear dresses or skirts to "make female players appear more feminine and appealing to fans and corporate sponsors," the *New York Times* reported at the time. "We just want them to look feminine and have a nice presentation so women will be more popular," said the federation's deputy president. (Thanks to the well-deserved uproar sparked by this dress code announcement, the federation backed off.)

Once again, it's two sides of the same coin. Either women are showing too much skin or they're showing too little skin. They are brazenly courting sexual attention or they're not giving audiences enough to ogle. And all this discourse is unrelated to what should be the focus, which is *how they play the sport*. The line of what counts as "acceptable" public dress is so thin and shifting that it's no wonder many women have decided they're simply not interested in trying to walk it anymore.

What's behind this ugly refusal to let women make their own decisions about how to dress on the court, or in society more broadly? Surprise,

surprise: It's misogyny! Most sports' international-governing bodies are full of powerful men who decide what women should wear and how they should be.

There is still a ways to go; however, in recent years, thanks largely to women's activism, dress codes have been growing more and more accepting. It's not just the FIFA's and FIBA's moves to allow players to wear hijabs in games. In 2019, the Women's Tennis Association explicitly allowed players to wear leggings without a skirt during matches. In July 2021, around the same time as the Norwegian Beach Handball protest, the German women's gymnastics team proudly wore full-body unitards at the Tokyo Olympics. This wasn't breaking any rules, but it was breaking with custom: The team was tired of the oversexualization of gymnasts in revealing leotards.

Taking sports away from anyone because of how they choose to dress and express themselves spiritually or culturally is unjust. Seeing more and more women rise to the highest levels of sports while dressing according to their own values—and seeing their sports' governing bodies accept their whole personhood—gives me hope for the future. When Nouhaila Benzina took to the pitch in Melbourne in August of 2023 at the Women's World Cup, I was in Australia to cover the tournament. Watching her on the field, at the top of her game, the first woman ever to wear a hijab at the Women's World Cup, was something I'll never forget. *This is what change looks like.*

"I AM LUCKY THAT WHATEVER FEAR I HAVE INSIDE ME, MY DESIRE TO WIN IS ALWAYS STRONGER."

Serena Williams

They Resist

IRANIAN WOMEN ATHLETES AND SOCCER FANS REWRITE THE RULES OF ENGAGEMENT

By Saeedeh Fathi in collaboration with Egab

It felt like the only choice, but that didn't mean it was an easy one. Nasim pulled back her hair in a tight, low bun; she fitted the wig, tucking each stray strand underneath a thick tuft of straight, black, short hair; she agonized over the moustache design and the length of her beard.

It was difficult, becoming a man.

Nasim, thirty, who asks that her identity remain concealed for fear of reprisal, is a Tehran resident. Born in Lahijan, an ancient city on the shores of the Caspian Sea known for producing fine silk, Nasim is no ordinary soccer fan. She would do whatever it takes to achieve her dream of being in the bleachers at Azadi Stadium to cheer for Persepolis against Tractor Sazi that day in 2018. Even disguise herself as a man.

"My friends were all against it," said Nasim. "It's too dangerous, they said, but I was thinking nobody would ever guess a woman would dare try to get in."

She remembers how she trembled when she approached the gate, "as if there was an earthquake." But her disguise worked. Three more times after that, she snuck into the stadium in disguise.

Ironically, *azadi* is a Persian word for "freedom." Yet Persian women are not free to enter the stadium bearing that name—or any stadium in Iran.

Left: Iranian soccer fans at Azadi Stadium in 2019

Maryam, thirty, who also prefers to remain anonymous, is another die-hard fan of Persepolis, like her mother before her. When the team was scheduled to face off against Foolad Khuzestan at Al-Ghadir Stadium in Ahvaz in January 2017, she knew what she had to do.

Maryam too risked everything, but she says it was all worth it.

"I never thought I'd feel so safe in the stadium. The men who knew I'm a woman wanted to protect me," she said.

She had a mini panic attack when a cheerleader asked why she wasn't cheering loud enough. "I was about to break out in laughter, but I held it in!"

But the absurdity of having to go through all this just to enter a stadium was no laughing matter, and it took a tragedy of colossal proportions to wake the world up to the injustice of it all.

Sahar Khodayari, the "Blue Girl"—a reference to her favorite team's jersey color—was only twenty-nine when she made the ultimate sacrifice. In 2019, she doused herself in gasoline and set herself on fire in front of a revolutionary court in Tehran.

Sahar had just learned that she was likely to face six months in prison for attempting to enter Azadi Stadium disguised as a man. She had gone to watch an AFC Champions League match between her favorite team, Esteghlal FC, and Al Ain. She had done this several times before, but this time she was caught and was held in jail for five days before being released on bail. She was charged with openly committing a "sinful act" by not covering her hair with a hijab.

A week later, she died in the hospital due to third-degree burns.

Since Sahar's heartbreaking suicide, female Iranian soccer fans have been allowed to cheer for their favorite soccer teams in the stadium only intermittently, at the whim of the authorities. Female fans made it to the Tehran Football Derby in Azadi Stadium for the first time in about a year—minus fake beards—on December 14, 2023. Even then, they were allocated only three thousand of the eighty-seven thousand available seats.

For the past four decades, women and girls have been banned from attending sports events in stadiums, not because there are laws prohibiting the pernicious crime of soccer fandom perpetrated by half the population, but because male authorities, comfortably perched on their moral high horses, claimed stadiums lacked the proper infrastructure to separate men from women.

And for the crime of attempting to breach this ridiculous ban, women were subjected to threats, arrest, detention, and jail. Even Sahar's self-immolation in protest at the discriminatory rules did not immediately impact the authorities, nor did numerous demands from FIFA that Iran end the stadium ban.

But if you think the fans had it bad, wait until I tell you about the Iranian women's soccer team—the Lionesses.

Yes, Iran has a women's team, which you probably never hear about except when there's breaking news that a player was forced to pass on a major international cup because her husband refused to issue an exit permit allowing her to travel. This is what happened in 2015 to Niloofar Ardalan, the team captain at the time. She missed the AFC Women's Futsal Championship in Malaysia—what would have been the crowning achievement in her nineteen-year career as a soccer player. By law, married women in Iran must get their husband's permission to travel abroad unless the husband has relinquished this power in the marriage contract.

Women's soccer in Iran started in the early 1970s, yet the team didn't play its first international match until 2005. And before you entertain any false notions about the Iranian federation's love of women's soccer, here's the sad truth: It was pressure from FIFA, which stipulates that member federations must officially recognize women soccer players and teams, that forced their hand, basically to save the Iranian men's team from expulsion. But the official nod didn't protect the women's team from neglect, as matches were scheduled at the worst times with virtually no media coverage.

No one knows that struggle better than the national team's current captain, Zahra Ghanbari. They call her the Cristiano of women in Iran. The nickname energizes her, she says.

Now thirty-two, Zahra wasn't always known as Cristiano—or even as Zahra. Like the fans who stuck fake beards on their faces for the love of the game, when she was six, Zahra dressed like a boy to play street soccer. Going through life as Ali Agha, she joined the local boys' soccer team. She pushed, she fell and got dirty, and everyone believed it, until one day her double life fell apart.

When the coach asked for her birth certificate, she broke down in tears, so her father agreed to reveal the truth to the coach and implore him to take her in. More awed by her exceptional talent than upset about her deceit, the coach wished he could help but said his hands were tied.

For years Zahra waited until the fields finally opened for women. She first played with Paykan FC in 2006. In 2007, at fifteen, she was invited to the national team, and in the same year she was named best player in the league and became the first Iranian woman soccer player to become a legionnaire, playing in Iraq. Back home in the 2018–2019 season, she scored a record fifty-one goals with Bam Khatoon FC.

Though she no longer needs to dress like a boy or change her name, the midfielder, forward, and defender still feels the discrimination.

"In the early years, people didn't know women's soccer existed," she said. "It was painful to hear people question our right to play and to wonder if we even exist as a team. They ask: Can women really run in those clothes and hijab? Can women tackle? When you see all the effort you're putting in, but no one knows about you, it's demotivating. Compared to men, we have nothing. In other countries women are fighting for equal salaries, but in Iran, we don't even have facilities to train. Our uniforms, like our contracts, are of poor quality."

Female soccer fans lack opportunities to play, to spectate, and even to do their jobs. In 2018, sports photographer Parisa Pourtaherian, who was twenty-six at the time, fought back with a massive telephoto lens. Determined to cover a match between Nassaji Mazandaran (one of Iran's oldest clubs) and Zob Ahan Esfahan FC, in Vatani Stadium in the northern city of Qaem Shahr, she started knocking on the doors of houses in the vicinity when the guards refused her entry.

"That day, on the rooftop of a nearby house whose owners allowed me in halfway through the match, I was thinking: *What's the difference between me and my male colleagues? Why can't I do my job when they can so easily do it?*" she recalls.

The twisted logic behind the ban is complicated even more by the random implementation.

Parisa is bewildered. "My female colleagues and I aren't allowed into soccer stadiums, but volleyball courts are accessible. They think we're pretending to be photographers just to watch the match. Women photographers aren't taken seriously," she says.

But none of it stopped her. Parisa became the first female Iranian photographer to find the perfect vantage point to cover a top-flight national league match. Both her photos and photos *of* her went viral, chipping away at the stadium ban and embarrassing its enforcers.

Moral of the story: For every mountain, there's a rooftop.

Philosopher Jacques Derrida, an avid soccer fan, once said: "Beyond the touchline, there is nothing."

As interpreted by journalist Shirsho Dasgupta, Derrida's sentiment wasn't saying that soccer is superior to every other aspect of life; he was saying that "everything that happens outside the stadium—politics, economics, or even art and culture—is automatically reflected inside it. The soccer pitch is a microcosm of life itself."

Soccer, he believed, reflects, and is an extension of, the nation.

In Iran, governmental policies toward women soccer players, journalists, and fans reflect policies toward women in general.

It takes guts to be a sports journalist in Iran. In the early 2000s, I was one of only a handful of women working in the field, and even though this has changed over the years, the path was full of thorns. Starting in 2021, under pressure from FIFA, a small number of women journalists were allowed to attend matches, but here's the catch: They're allowed no access to mixed-gender zones or the press conference area. Instead, they're placed in a glass room. Yes, you read that right. It's as if the Iranian government learned the concept of a glass ceiling and thought, *Great idea, but I bet we can take it even further.*

I've been a journalist for more than twenty years, but I've never been allowed to watch a match live in the stadium in my own country. In trying, I have been clubbed, tear-gassed, and forced to cover myself with a chador. In February 2018, I was detained for a full day because I dared

In Iran, governmental policies toward women soccer players, journalists, and fans reflect policies toward women in general.

attempt to cover the final game of the Iranian Basketball Super League inside the court.

None of this stopped me. I was arrested in October 2022 while covering the Women, Life, Freedom movement that erupted after the tragic death of Mahsa Amini. Amini died in a hospital in Tehran soon after she was arrested and allegedly abused by religious morality police for not wearing her hijab in accordance with government standards. Her death sparked widespread protests and a social media trend of Iranian women recording themselves cutting off their hair. I was detained for two months in Tehran's notorious Evin Prison for doing my job: giving voice to hundreds of women athletes and exposing the injustice of the bans and limitations Iranian women have struggled against for decades.

It's hard to find a silver lining in any of this when I remember Melika Mohammadi, the dedicated member of the national team who left her life behind in the United States to pursue her dream of playing in Iran.

She was twenty-three and she is dead. Melika, an Iranian American who previously played for Emory University, was a defender born in Shiraz, Iran, who went on to play for Bam Khatoon FC. She represented Iran five times during the 2022 AFC Women's Asian Cup qualifiers.

But none of it mattered. She was killed in a taxi accident on her way home from training on December 24, 2023. This was not an act of God. It was neglect. Clubs don't provide safe transport for their women's teams, even while they shower their male counterparts with latest model luxury cars.

Melika's teammates participated in a lap of honor to commemorate her in Azadi. The crowds in Iran's biggest stadium cheered for her. This was the first time that Azadi, the supposed "freedom" stadium, had ever hosted such a tribute for a female athlete. The dream came true, but only to honor her deceased body.

So, is there a silver lining?

No. Perhaps. Maybe.

Ultimately every act of resistance is a ray of hope. I think of Sahar, Parisa, Zahra, Melika, Maryam, Nasim, and the thousands of other Iranian women, loud and proud, breaking out of their glass rooms one little bit at a time.

Now, that's a silver lining.

"IF YOU
CAN CHANGE ONE
PERSON'S LIFE,
THAT'S ALL
YOU CAN ASK FOR.
BUT IF YOU
CAN IMPACT MANY,
EVEN BETTER."

Sue Bird

She Cheers for Herself First

JUSTINE LINDSAY, NFL CHEERLEADER

By Frankie de la Cretaz

In 2022, the ranks of NFL cheerleaders got a new member: Justine Lindsay. The then-twenty-nine-year-old dancer who made the Carolina Panthers' TopCats cheer squad had the moves, the rhythm, and the high jumps. She was also making history: Justine was officially the first openly transgender woman to cheer in the NFL.

At the Panthers' home opener at Bank of America Stadium on September 11, Justine was all smiles. "It was the best moment I could imagine," she told NFL.com of being on the field during the game. "It felt like it was about 115 degrees and there were so many people in the stands. It was a beautiful Sunday."

The milestone was significant for a number of reasons. Firstly, cheerleading has always been seen as the ultimate purview of feminine, conventionally attractive women—think the line of near-identical thin, blonde-haired white women doing high kicks on the sidelines of games as seen on the show *Dallas Cowboys Cheerleaders: Making the Team*. Think, while you're at it, of pretty much any movie or TV show set in high school.

As a Black transgender woman rocking a bald head, Justine showcases beauty and dance skills that challenge the long-held image of what kind of woman could be an NFL cheerleader. Black women are still in the minority among NFL cheerleaders—though the TopCats are one of the most racially diverse teams in the league, with at least half the squad being women of color—and a trans cheerleader was unheard of until Justine came along. Which is why she wanted to usher in a new era for NFL cheerleading, she told *ELLE* magazine, one in which "it's okay to be your most authentic self."

But it's even bigger than that too. Justine entered the NFL during a time of heightened attention—and danger—for trans people in the United States, both in sports and in the world at large. In 2022, the same year that Justine joined the TopCats, more than three hundred anti-LGBTQ+ bills were introduced in state legislatures. Anti-trans legislation that is designed to push transgender people out of public life has come in the form of bans on trans people using bathrooms or locker rooms that don't match the sex they were assigned at birth; bans on gender-affirming health care for children and potentially adults as well; and restrictions targeting transgender athletes—transgender women, in particular.

Not only that, but violence against transgender people has been an epidemic in the United States. In 2022, thirty-two trans people were killed—the overwhelming majority of whom were Black transgender women. Shortly before Justine joined the TopCats, two transgender women were found murdered in a hotel room not far from the Panthers' stadium.

In other words, being a trans person in America comes with risks. This is especially true for hypervisible trans people with platforms, like Justine. But with that platform also comes the potential to have a significant positive impact. "Everything that I'm going through now, it's bigger than me," Justine told *ELLE*. "I'm setting things up for the younger generation. No one is going to stop this show."

Justine made the intentional choice to share her identity with the world. In an interview with BuzzFeed News, she said that before she announced on Instagram that she'd made the TopCats squad, very few people in her life outside of her family members knew she was transgender—not even her best friends. "I just felt like when I posted it, whatever reaction I get from everyone, it does not matter," Justine told BuzzFeed News. "And then my phone started blowing up."

Justine grew up in the Charlotte, North Carolina, suburb of Dilworth, about two miles from Bank of America Stadium, where she now performs during Panthers' home games. Her father played college football and hoped she would play the sport, too, but her mother enrolled her in ballet classes instead. Ultimately, Justine's love of dance would provide her with the skills to eventually find her way onto the field of the sport her father loved so much. Football gameday is such a part of American culture, and many women who are shut out of the game on the field, or are not interested in playing the contact sport, access gameday culture through other means—as fans, commentators, and cheerleaders.

Since their start in the 1950s, NFL cheer squads have traditionally been the realm of conventionally pretty—and often scantily clad—young women. As a job for women, pro cheerleading has come with a host of indignities, often including low pay, restrictive rules (including requirements for weight and hair), and sexual harassment.

"Everything that I'm going through now, it's bigger than me."

In recent years, however, various NFL squads have made headlines for adding male cheerleaders. In 2019, professional dancers Quinton Peron and Napoleon Jinnies made the Los Angeles Rams' cheerleading team—and then took their historic season all the way to the Super Bowl, where they became the first male cheerleaders to be on the field at the championship game. But until Justine came along, no openly trans women had ever been on the sidelines.

From a young age, Justine excelled at dance. She told *ELLE* that she was first exposed to the art when she was just five years old and the Alvin Ailey American Dance Theater came to town with their show *Revelations*. "Seeing people that looked like me . . . and how they were able to move their bodies, well, it really stuck with me," Justine said. "I was like, 'Dang, I could do that.'"

When she was fourteen, Justine received a scholarship to attend the Debbie Allen Dance Academy in Los Angeles. She moved across the country by herself and relished the opportunity to be surrounded by other passionate dancers and artists. "I was around people who were open about being who they are," she told *ELLE*. That openness provided the space for her to interrogate who she was too. And that's when, at eighteen years old, she understood that she "was always Justine."

In 2016, she graduated from North Carolina State University with a degree in communications and moved back to Charlotte. She began to meet other Black trans women through the local community and found the ballroom circuit, which she loved. She researched her community's history, watching films like the 1990 documentary *Paris Is Burning*, and came into her identity more fully. And a key part of that identity always had been, and always would be, dancing. A new friend suggested she try out for the TopCats. Despite being nervous, Justine decided to go for it.

The NFL is not a league known for progressive values. This is especially true in states like North Carolina, where the Panthers are based, which went for Republican candidate Donald Trump in both the 2016 and 2020 presidential elections. The Panthers fan base ranked twenty-second out of thirty-two teams in a FiveThirtyEight study of how liberal NFL fan bases are. In 2023, the North Carolina legislature also passed a rash of anti-trans legislation, in some cases overriding their governor's veto in order to do so.

"We are in the South," TopCats squad member Chris Crawford told *ELLE*, "and there are gender norms and trends that aren't always recognized, accepted, or acknowledged."

For as long as openly trans women have been participating in women's sports, detractors have complained of their supposedly unfair physiological advantages. "Bans on trans athletes, especially those that focus on trans women and girls, have benefited for years from being framed by their partisans as more reasonable, or perhaps *the only* reasonable form of anti-trans discrimination," Jules Gill-Peterson, associate professor of history at Johns Hopkins University, who specializes in transgender history, wrote in her Substack newsletter, Sad Brown Girl.

"They invoke the platitude of 'fairness' in competition, the genuine history of women's unequal access to participation, and an ostensibly scientific conversation about sex differences and their relationship to athletic capacity."

Luckily Justine has had the full support of her teammates as well as her coaches. "My goal is to create a team of individuals that are absolute fire on the field but are incredible human beings in the locker room, good friends, good people, and at the end of the day, you have to walk through the door first to get to that spot," Chandalae Lanouette, the TopCats' director, told BuzzFeed News.

Chandalae also made it clear that Justine's talent is what earned her a place on the squad. "She had a shaved head and so much confidence," Chandalae told *ELLE*. In addition to being "ridiculously talented," she said that Justine had "so much joy in performing."

That doesn't mean life as a professional cheerleader is always easy for Justine. She has dealt with digital harassment and mean comments online—all the bullshit you'd expect. And while having the support of her coaches and teammates, the Panthers organization, and her family and friends is great, there are days when Justine says the trolling gets to her. How could it not? But she recognizes that what she's doing is bigger than her.

"Being out on the field on Sundays representing [the Panthers] organization is more than me just being a cheerleader," she told NFL.com. "It's being a face of the possible. I never thought I would have this much courage to do this."

She Opens Doors

RANI RAMPAL, QUEEN OF THE FIELD

By Deepti Patwardhan

If you were a sports fan in India in the 1990s, cricket dominated your world. The sport was all over TV and newspapers. Little thought or space was given to other sports. Every four years, when the Summer Olympics came along, India would turn in dismal results. The country won zero medals at the 1992 Summer Olympics in Barcelona, and one each in the next three. Which meant India was firmly planted last in the medals-to-population ratio.

But these days, athletes from tiny, dusty, forgotten towns, which lie on the fringes of the technological and economic boom of urban India, are finding their identity through sports. Women, despite being given a laundry list of reasons not to play, are at the forefront of that change. They are crashing through the walls of convention built around them by a deeply patriarchal society.

One person who embodies the struggle is Rani Rampal, captain of the Indian women's field hockey team that finished fourth at the 2020 Summer Olympics in Tokyo. Both Rani and her team traveled further than anyone expected of them, on roads that they built themselves.

Born on December 4, 1994, Rani is the third and youngest child in her family. Her name is Sanskrit for "queen." Three generations and seven members of the family—Rani's grandparents, her parents, and her two brothers—lived in a tiny mud dwelling in the town of Shahabad Markanda, Haryana, India. Her father earned his livelihood by transporting goods on a horse-drawn cart and picking up odd jobs, bringing home 80 Indian rupees (INR) or approximately $1 per day.

In the evenings after school, Rani would spend her time on the sidelines of a local playground, watching girls play field hockey. Shahabad Markanda is only a tiny town, but its claim to fame in India is women's hockey. It has produced more than forty international players. Fascinated by the game, in which crouched players dribble the ball with curved sticks, Rani wanted to join in. But her family struggled to eat three square meals a day—they didn't have the resources to buy her hockey gear. When Rani's father did take her to try out at the local academy, the coach was reluctant to take her on since she was undernourished.

The bigger battle that she had to face, however, wasn't financial. It was reputational. Her parents, who never had access to education, were taunted by their friends and relatives for letting their daughter play a sport.

In the years Rani was growing up, the state of Haryana had one of the highest rates of female feticide in India, and, naturally, a skewed sex ratio. Women had little to no freedom to pursue their ambitions. Not only stepping outside the house but even *wanting* to step outside was frowned upon. Rani's parents' friends and family encouraged them to prevent their daughter from playing hockey. Why? Because she would have to wear shorts. By stepping out of the house, onto the playground, and going out to play matches and tournaments, she would befoul the family name. She was seven years old at the time.

Unfortunately, this has been a regular theme with Indian sportswomen over the years, a common story of girls' uncles and aunties judging them for pursuing their passions. Girls in towns, villages, and even conservative families in cities are expected to stay at home, dress modestly, master household chores, get married when they turn the legal age of eighteen, and start a family. With little to no social and financial freedom, decisions are made for them by their fathers, grandfathers, or male guardians, and later by their husbands.

But Rani was not so easily dissuaded. Before she was ten, she decided to take charge of her life.

"At that time, I thought playing hockey [was] the only way to change my circumstances. If I don't play hockey, maybe my life won't change," she says. "It wasn't strictly a matter of choice. Hockey was the only popular sport in my town. I wasn't sure whether or not my parents would have the means to support my education. In rural areas, usually they put girls through school till grade ten then get them married off. Hockey was the only path available; I made it my path."

When Rani did join the hockey academy, she played in a salwar kameez (traditional baggy pants and long top) and white canvas shoes, which cost 60 INR. The coach provided her with a secondhand, weathered hockey stick. One of the coach's rules was that the kids drink 500 milliliters of milk after their training. Since her family didn't even have 500 milliliters for the entire household, Rani would add water to 200 milliliters of milk and take it to training.

Practice started at five in the morning, but the family didn't own an alarm clock. Her mother would spend sleepless nights anxious about getting up in time to get little Rani ready and drop her off at training. But Rani had a solution to this. Every year, a handwriting competition was held at Rani's school, and the winner would get an alarm clock as a prize. Rani practiced handwriting every day to ensure she won the competition and the clock so her mother could sleep peacefully. *Jugaad*, she calls it. Hustle.

Rani's tough upbringing instilled in her a sense of discipline. She had seen her father toil all hours in all seasons, in searing heat and in freezing cold, and that inspired her work ethic. Having started off as a midfielder, Rani quickly rose to prominence as a forward. She was a natural predator in front of the goal, with a built-in radar to be in the right place at the right time.

She was so good that she made it to the junior national camp when she was eleven—but her stint was cut short by a brutal back injury.

"The national coach there asked me to squat with an 80-kilogram weight," remembers Rani. "At that time, my weight was 36 kilograms. I told him I won't be able to pick up such a big weight. He said, if you can't, you put it in writing and submit that to the federation." Worried that saying no would lead to her dismissal, Rani did as she was told. Only the weight, as she had presumed, was too heavy for her. It fell on her back and led to an injury that she still hasn't been able to shake off completely.

Even now, Rani has to put in two extra hours a day on her body, doing more motion exercises and recovery sessions to keep the pain at bay. The pain is exacerbated by playing; in hockey, players spend most of their time on the field in a bent, crouched position and have to swiftly twist and turn to dribble and shoot. Rani's infuriatingly preventable injury highlights the lack of training and apathy of the system that was supposed to prepare young athletes.

After her injury, Rani took a year to get back on the hockey field. But she *did* get back. Rani reemerged on the domestic scene in 2007—this time straight into the senior national camp.

At fourteen, she became the youngest player to represent India in women's hockey as she competed in the Olympic qualifiers in Kazan, Russia, in 2008. Until then, Rani didn't know that women's hockey was even on the Olympic roster. At that point, India's women's team had participated only once in the Olympics, at the 1980 Moscow Games.

"We didn't do too well in that tournament," Rani recalls of the 2008 qualifiers. "I remember the senior players crying their eyes out. I didn't completely understand the emotion then." But four years later, she felt it herself. "The qualifying tournament for the 2012 London Olympics was held in India, and we lost the final to South Africa. That was when it hit me. I sat outside my hotel room for almost the whole night and cried. That's when I realized how important it was. So many great Indian players had come and gone without the chance of playing at the Olympics."

The unfulfilled ambition of generations of Indian players stung her. Like she had earlier in her life, Rani wanted to break the cycle. "I felt like if we can't do it either, who will?" Qualifying for the Olympics became her mission.

She made a major step toward that goal in 2013, when India clinched a bronze medal at the Women's Junior World Cup. It was their first podium finish at the world event. Many of the players on that team, including Rani—who was named the player of the tournament—are credited with launching the golden age of Indian women's hockey. Nine of them—Rani, Deep Grace Ekka, Sushila Chanu, Monika Malik, Navjot Kaur, Navneet Kaur, Namita Toppo, Vandana Katariya, and Lilima Minz—would go on to represent India at the Tokyo Games.

These athletes took India to the Olympics not just once but twice. They ended a thirty-six-year wait by qualifying for the 2016 Rio Games. But once there, the occasion overwhelmed them. India didn't win a single match and ended twelfth of twelve teams. It wasn't the result they were looking for, but the experience proved valuable. They needed the lessons from Rio to make Tokyo count.

In 2017, South Africa's Wayne Lombard was appointed the team's lead scientific advisor of athletic performance. Having worked with elite athletes in various sports, he came with a wealth of knowledge and a no-nonsense attitude. He quickly put the women to work on their speed, endurance, and strength. "We knew where we stood. Indian hockey was never short of skills," Rani says. "But we couldn't compete with the European teams due to the physicality. They would push and shove." Until Lombard's arrival, the hockey team always packed that extra baggage of an inferiority complex when they traveled to tournaments.

Lombard brought modern training methods, cranked up the intensity, and tweaked diets according to individual needs. They had come a long way since the length of their sports outfits was a matter of censure; what mattered now was the life in their legs and definition of muscle.

"When we started seeing the changes the improved fitness was bringing on the field, they were running easily, they felt strong on the ball," says Rani. "Once we started competing with Australian teams, European teams, when they pushed [us] we would also push back. We started feeling confident. This was practical hockey."

Even as they improved, the women's hockey team was treated like an afterthought. The reminders of how little they mattered were constant. For example, Sjoerd Marijne, brought in as head coach of the Indian women's hockey team in February 2017, was handed the role of guiding the men's team instead in September. After the Indian men's team finished a disappointing fourth at the 2018 Commonwealth Games, Marijne was sent back to the women's team. Are you keeping up? With the blatant sexism?

Being treated as some sort of consolation prize only strengthened the sisterhood within the team. Rani's teammates all had their unique struggles to get there: Neha Goyal had found the solace of hockey in a home where her father would turn up drunk and assault her mother; fiery forward Vandana Katariya faced financial struggles early on and contemplated suicide in 2009 after she was dropped from the national camp; Salima

Tete, who tears through the wing, started life in hockey on uneven, rocky ground using hockey sticks fashioned out of bamboo sticks, belonging to the tribal belt in India's eastern state of Jharkhand. A lack of respect from the country's governing bodies was not going to deflate them easily. These women had already stared down bigger odds in life and overcome them. What India now had was a bunch of fine-tuned, hungry athletes hell-bent on making a stir.

Going into the 2020 Summer Olympics in Tokyo, which were deferred to 2021, India's women's team was ranked ninth in the world. They started their Olympic run with three straight defeats. "Everyone thought our Olympics [was] over," says Rani. "But we backed ourselves." In their fourth group match, India beat Ireland 1–0 to stay afloat in the tournament. Then they scored a 4–3 win over South Africa, and Katariya scored India's first hat trick at the Olympics to sneak into the quarterfinals.

The team's legend was forged under the blazing sun in Tokyo as they outran, outpaced, and out-endured three-time Olympic champions Australia. The only goal of the match came from Gurjit Kaur, India's first real specialist drag-flicker. And with that, India's women's hockey team made it to the semifinals, a place no one had ever expected them to be.

India lost the semifinals to Argentina and suffered a heartbreaking 3–4 defeat to Great Britain in the bronze medal playoff. But they had defied all expectations to finish in the final four. Beyond India, beyond hockey, they were underdogs showing viewers around the world how a team of unstoppable women could create opportunity out of nothing.

"Before Tokyo, I had never seen Indians wake up early [in the] morning to watch not cricket, but women's hockey," Rani says. "From the very beginning, what I wanted to do was open doors for women. Sport[s] changed my life. I had never imagined life could be like this. Hockey has given me everything. Not only financially. But it has given me identity. It has given me a voice."

> "From the very beginning, what I wanted to do was open doors for women."

"IF YOU JUST
PUSH THROUGH
THE STRUGGLES
AND THE HARD
TIMES, IT'LL BE SO
WORTH IT IN
THE END, BECAUSE
YOU WILL
BE ABLE TO GET TO
YOUR DREAMS."

Chloe Kim

She Builds a Legacy

MAYBELLE BLAIR CAME OUT TO PLAY BALL

By Mollie Cahillane

The 1992 classic *A League of Their Own* is required viewing for sports fans. While everyone remembers the epic final scene between sisters Kit and Dottie, fewer know the name Maybelle Blair, the woman who inspired the film that brought the Rockford Peaches and the phrase "There's no crying in baseball!" into the mainstream.

Ninety-seven-year-old Maybelle Blair is one of the few living original members of the All-American Girls Professional Baseball League, which existed from 1943 to 1954. The former pitcher for the Peoria Redwings became a baseball player by intention and a star by circumstance. Recently an adviser for Amazon Prime Video's *A League of Their Own* series, Maybelle has left an indelible impact on the game.

In 2022, Maybelle walked into a Tribeca Film Festival panel in New York City with executive producers of the show Abbi Jacobson and Will Graham. Holding a baseball bat transformed into a walking cane, Maybelle came out of the closet, where she'd been for nearly all her ninety-five years. She'd had no intention of publicly coming out as gay at that panel, but, quite emotionally, she did. And since then, her already remarkable legacy has grown beyond anything she could have imagined.

Now the former player is out and proud, and working to give girls in baseball a place where they belong, one just as significant as her own.

That place is the International Women's Baseball Center, located in Rockford, Illinois. Seventy years ago, this was the home field for the Rockford Peaches, one of the founding teams in the All-American Girls Professional Baseball League. Part museum, part ballpark, part community, the IWBC will—Maybelle hopes—cement the future of the sport for young women around the world.

As children in Southern California, the only things Maybelle and her brothers had for entertainment were a bat, a ball, and a baseball field, which they built themselves. The family wrapped their balls and bats in tape to keep them together because "we didn't have any money for anything else."

"I had to play baseball, or I would've been thrown into the ocean," Maybelle joked, recalling life in a family of ballplayers. "But, boy, could we play ball. I don't ever remember not playing baseball."

The future professional spent time in front of a radio, keeping baseball scores for her brothers. She learned how to keep a scorebook by the time she was six years old, following the Chicago Cubs on the radio station out in Los Angeles.

She recalled going to Sears around Christmastime. Santa Claus was giving out dolls and balls. The baseball star remembered that when she won a raffle at the event, the dressed-up Kriss Kringle automatically assumed she wanted a doll, not a ball.

"I started crying. I said, 'Mom, I wanted a ball, not a damn doll,'" said Maybelle. "I was so heartbroken—but then I got my ball."

Maybelle's entire family on both sides always played baseball, and once the All-American Girls Baseball League started, it was a "no-brainer" for her.

After being drafted to the professional league in 1948, Maybelle was "thrilled to death," although she says it was a "shame" that a war had brought on the opportunity.

"Who would ever think I was ever going to be able to play baseball, because women just didn't do anything," said Maybelle. "Only thing we could do was either be a schoolteacher, nurse, or a secretary, and that was about it."

"I thought I was the cutest girl God ever made," she said, about putting on her professional uniform for the first time.

"I turned the corner and I saw the field and the green grass, and I said, 'Oh, Maybelle, you're a professional baseball player.'"

Fans of the film and streaming series *A League of Their Own* will remember the iconic moments when the stars see the Chicago baseball field for the first time as players in uniform. But for Maybelle, that was a real-life experience.

"I got my dress on, and I put on my cleats. I was getting nervous, and I put on those as I started walking. [There's] nothing more music in the world than that clickety-clack against a hard surface with cleats on. I had that clickety-clack, and then I turned the corner and I saw the field and the green grass, and I said, 'Oh, Maybelle, you're a professional baseball player.'"

She played one season for the Redwings and then moved on to a professional softball career in Chicago before entering a thirty-seven-year-long career at the aerospace and defense technology company Northrop Corporation. There, she started as a chauffeur before becoming one of the first female managers of the company.

Now the IWBC is her primary focus.

"The girls who want to play baseball, they're just left out. And it's a crying shame they haven't had a chance to play, and that's why we're trying so hard to build a home in Rockford, Illinois," Maybelle said. "We do not belong in the Hall of Fame in Cooperstown due to the fact that we haven't earned it, and we never will. We'll never be able to compete with men; we don't *want* to compete with men. We need a home of our own and a league of our own.

"When little girls come to Rockford and play, tears come to their eyes because they played where the Rockford Peaches played, and it's so amazing."

The eventual goal for Maybelle is to develop a Hall of Fame where All-Americans can become members but so can ballplayers from countries like Japan, Australia, and Canada.

"They are so far ahead of us right now; we've got to get moving," said Maybelle of these other nations. "We're just dragging our feet, and we're not getting enough support. We've got to get that place built so that people will start understanding how important it is to the women."

The idea for the International Women's Baseball Center came years ago, but according to Maybelle, folks at the time were not listening to legends like herself and fellow members of the original league.

Back in 2014, Maybelle helped form a committee to launch the IWBC in Rockford. The group secured the property across the street from the original Beyer Stadium, where the Peaches played in the 1940s and '50s.

But her ambitions don't stop with the IWBC. She also plans to launch another women's baseball league in the United States, hopefully within the next two years—that is to say, before she turns one hundred.

Maybelle is hesitant to launch too early, however, noting that without a complete product, the league will not have staying power.

"People will come to see it for a novelty, but if it's not completely good enough, they're not going to waste their money," she said. "And it costs money to be able to have a league of their own."

For Maybelle, that means at least four good teams to launch. The former power pitcher believes the United States could currently field two and a half good teams. But she also believes we'll get to four.

She hopes that the renewed spotlight on *A League of Their Own* will help her achieve that goal by driving girls' attention to baseball once again. And it doesn't hurt that she went viral for coming out after the series premiered.

Serving as an adviser for the show, Maybelle hoped to authentically reflect the experience of queer women in the original league. But she didn't plan to identify publicly as gay, especially as she wasn't out to her family or to her former employers.

But after spending decades in the closet, she finally felt comfortable enough to be her authentic self, especially after seeing Jacobson and Graham publicly out.

"They were asking me questions [about my experience], and I was trying to answer as many as I could without coming out and saying I was gay or anything like that, and I think they realized I was," said Maybelle.

"I had to be in the closet with the job I had; I had to watch my p's and q's, or I would have been fired right on the spot," she said.

During her impromptu speech at Tribeca, Maybelle said she had known she'd liked women since high school, but she initially felt like she was the only person in the world who felt that way.

"I hid for seventy-five or eighty-five years, and this is basically the first time I've ever come out," the player said at the time, telling a crowd giving her a standing ovation that there is a life for queer women and to follow it.

The star credits the environment Graham and Jacobson created while she served as a series adviser for helping her feel comfortable enough to publicly live her true self.

"Everybody knows Abbi; I haven't heard anybody talk about her being gay or Will being gay. I said to myself, 'Maybelle, you don't have to worry about Northrop anymore or any of your jobs or anything like that. Who are you worried about? My God, you're ninety-five years old. And you know, hey, you may be dead tomorrow—who knows, and who's gonna care anymore?'"

After her coming out, she had a conversation with her family confirming she was accepted, regardless of "what she does in the bedroom" or anything else.

"I haven't heard one negative word from anybody—probably behind my back, but not in front of me," joked Maybelle.

"All my blood went right clear down to my toes. I felt so relieved that it was out, after all those years of hiding it and worrying. You just can't imagine what a relief," she said.

"So many people have come up and told me how happy they are that I came out. It has made *me* feel so happy that I did have enough nerve to come out and tell people after all these years, and it was pent up in me so bad and I wanted to tell the world, but I just couldn't. Thank God for Abbi and Will—they were the two main ones who helped me come out. It was a perfect environment," said Maybelle.

As of now, she is back happily living in Southern California, chatting with me while sitting in her rocking chair overlooking the ocean. She hopes that the IWBC will be built before she passes, and she has promised to play catch with me the next time I venture to the West Coast.

Truly, Maybelle Blair is in a league of her own.

They Were the Few

FINDING THE FREEDOM TO JUST PLAY

By Lauren J. S. Porter

There's something that happens when Black people congregate in the same space. Looks are shared. Words are understood, even when they aren't uttered. A passing glance can translate into an entire conversation that can evoke a range of emotions that we can decipher with the tilt of the head.

Maybe it's an ancestral birthright that's innately passed down from one generation to the next. Or a lesson we picked up along the way when we knew we had to look to one another just to get by.

Whatever it is, it's magical.

But what happens when entering spaces and sports where you're one of the few people, or sometimes the only person, who look like you? Does it impact how you perform, how you compete, how you dominate? Does it discourage you from coming back, from trying to make room for yourself, from even walking in the door the first time?

For some? I'm sure.

As for the best in the game? Nothing can stop the greatness that goes into being a Black woman who has earned her roster spot in a traditionally white sport.

Left: Baylor Henry

Take Baylor Henry, for example, a collegiate student athlete who is now one of a handful of Black women on her crew team. But that wasn't always the reality for the Georgia native, who hails from Alpharetta, a northern suburb of Atlanta.

When Baylor first became interested in rowing, she often looked around and found herself being the only.

She transitioned into the sport from swimming, where her parents had invested in her learning not to be afraid of the water. They put her in lessons early on, immersing her in the pool, and followed her lead when she liked the sport. Eventually, that fun-loving focus on swimming led to her spot on the swim team.

But like many Black women, Baylor quickly learned that the chlorine in the pool water didn't play nice with the crowning glory that is our hair. She became determined to figure out how she could be *of* the water without being *in* the water.

Then she found rowing.

The summer before she started high school in 2017, she attended a camp dedicated to the sport. There, she felt comfort in looking around and seeing other girls her age, from similar backgrounds and with similar interests, gravitating toward an experience that would spawn new opportunities.

When the camp concluded, however, the diversity that Baylor found herself surrounded by at the start thinned out.

"I believe it was a commitment issue to the sport and also racial bias," she recalled as to why the start and end of her camp experience looked and felt so different. "Rowing is demanding and the lengths it takes to plan your day around crew practice, new hairstyles for the week, or coming home from being in the elements for two hours on the water in whatever kind of weather can be taxing. Let alone not seeing many Black athletes in the sport doing it or at least looking like they are enjoying what they are doing."

She realized she had fallen in love with a sport that would quickly introduce her to the biases, criticisms, differences, and politics that all too often discourage talented athletes of color from reaching their full potential.

"Some teammates on the women's and men's sides make snarky comments during sessions and often are fueled by the cultural differences between Black and white people. It ranged from comments of 'Why do they speak like that' or 'Why can't you wear your hair straight' to 'There are so many Black people here, what the heck.' Those are not inviting comments to join a team."

Baylor felt alone, navigating the waters of a new sport that culturally wasn't easy for her to access, let alone succeed in.

"During my time in high school crew, I experienced a double standard with the coaching staff. My self-doubt was fueled by the uncomfortable obstacles I was facing privately with the coaches. There would be countless moments where I simply didn't feel like I belonged because there was so much I had to prove. It felt like a test against my white teammates if I was built for the sport or not."

Despite all she experienced in high school, Baylor was dedicated to crew and is currently a member of her collegiate crew team.

So how did she put her best boat forward and eventually, at twenty years old, make history as she rowed in the first all-Black, all-female eight crew to compete at the Head Of The Charles Regatta, the world's largest three-day rowing competition?

She stayed the course, left her burdens on the shoreline, and set sail to achieve a groundbreaking feat. What she relied upon the most is the connection she has with the water, where things are serene and stable.

"The best feeling that I get is honestly a state of being in control of myself [and] being able to take the oar, literally row, and it's like gliding," Baylor recounts. "I'm able just to relax, enjoying the motions of the sport, and the beauty of it. The best feeling I get is one of I'm here. I get to do this; I actually have the opportunity to do this. Also knowing, wow, I can have a sense of control, of 'Okay, I can take it where I want without all the noise involved.'"

These sentiments are echoed by Hailey and Myla Barnett, fraternal twin sisters who also, elsewhere in the country, found themselves among the few in sports that aren't traditionally dominated, or even played, by many women who look like them.

Hailey, like Baylor, found herself drawn to rowing after competing as a swimmer. Myla took her talents from the pool to land, where she played lacrosse—a sport known for having a hefty price tag and not a lot of athletes of color on the field.

While the twins participated in two very different sports, a shared thread of their experiences was knowing how fortunate they were to participate.

"We feel very privileged and lucky to be given that opportunity [because we] know that the reason why a lot of Black and brown kids aren't in these predominantly white sports is not because of lack of talent, it's because of lack of exposure, a lot of the time," Hailey shares. "But our parents have always encouraged us that we can do whatever we want, do whatever we put our mind to, and there's no boundaries."

The Barnett twins know that part of their privilege lies in the foundation that their parents—a former NFL star father and a mother who was trained in classical ballet—created for them. They also know that their privilege comes with a responsibility, and it's one they don't take lightly.

Myla started on her collegiate lacrosse team during her senior year and saw success throughout the regular season and the ACC Women's Lacrosse Championship semifinals, but her goal wasn't just to win. It was also to open the door for younger athletes who look like her to follow her lead in the future.

"I certainly feel very honored. It's luck, but it's also when progress or hard work meets opportunity," says Myla.

That opportunity sometimes comes with an unspoken clause. There's certainly an unwavering pride felt when you are fortunate enough to fulfill your purpose—especially when you are one of the few to compete—but there's a cost too. It can be lonely and stressful, never being given the grace to mess up or have a bad day without worrying that you might be letting down younger athletes who look up to you or giving your doubters more ammunition.

How heavy it must be to just want to be a kid, to just want to play a sport, to just want to experience the joy that the game brings without having to worry about what the weight of your participation even means.

Hailey shared of her experience in crew, "In my eight years of rowing, I never experienced explicit bias or racism in the space of rowing; however, being one of the only Black girls on the team, I did put pressure on myself to be the point person for anyone's questions regarding race. The pressure to talk about race reached a height in 2020 with the murder of George Floyd and Breonna Taylor. I felt like I was expected to be the point person for my teammates and coaches on race relations. I minored in African

American studies, and I have always been interested in Black culture and amplifying the Black experience because it is one of my passions, but not every Black athlete on a predominantly white team should feel like the pressure falls on them to educate their team on racism in America."

Myla added, "When you think of a lacrosse team—all the white girls who were playing—there is somebody who's out there who's mentoring them, is coaching them, and that looks like them. They're reminded that it's possible and when you don't always have that, it doesn't feel as encouraging. To be able to be one of those faces, I was looking for that. To be able to see somebody who [looked like me] that was doing it and killing it, it's a really good feeling and you feel motivated by that. Even when we played other teams, and there were those few Black girls, we knew to say, 'What's up?' And understanding that, if they're having the best game, of course, I'm going to play defense, but it doesn't go unnoticed when you're one of the few, if not the only one."

See? That unspoken magic shows up even when the other person who looks like you is on the opposing side. And it's the same magic that helps you form connective bonds with those around you—and, when the stars align, it can even help you make history.

When Baylor first competed at the Head Of The Charles in 2019, she didn't know what to expect. "I remember just calling my parents, concerned and worried because I was also the only person of color that made

"Not every Black athlete on a predominantly white team should feel like the pressure falls on them to educate their team on racism in America."

Hailey Barnett and her crew

it to go to Head Of The Charles. I remember looking around and just feeling so out of place because nobody looked like me at all."

Three years later, in 2022, she returned to the prestigious competition—but this time, that feeling of loneliness wasn't there. This time the magic met Baylor.

With the help of *Rowing in Color*, a podcast that began in 2020 to amplify rowers of color, Baylor and seven other athletes formed Head Of The Charles's first all-Black women's eight.

"When I received the invitation from *Rowing in Color* to stroke the first all-Black women's eight, I was curious to see if things had changed in three years. Upon my arrival to the course, I was pleasantly surprised. There was a greater level of diversity than in my first experience. The women in the lineup were women I connected with online, so I had known and highlighted them on my social page, Black Girls Row.

"It was a surreal moment to come back and be with women who look like me—[some] have competed in the Olympics, [others] have gone to [great] schools—that was so amazing. We all were able to discuss our experiences and just the reality of what we were doing. Seeing an all-Black women's eight on the water is just something you don't see. I knew the weight of that [and] it was just such a beautiful performance. It was just like, 'Yeah, we can do it too, and we're powerful.' So nobody can say anything against that."

Baylor continued, "Universally, as a Black woman, we all know that feeling like you have to prove something more than what other people do. Being there, [and gaining] that community, I hope I've shown and pioneered that, especially with my story of even being able to participate at Head Of The Charles, and being in the first all-Black women's eight. The struggles that we all [in] the sport have experienced, especially the biases, the coaching staff, and just even your teammates, it's really unfortunate. But knowing that, hey, that does not stop you. You're not limited to that. There is more beyond that. Hopefully what I have been able to cultivate can help navigate that for the younger girls that are going to do it [in the future]."

Baylor has never met twins and former college athletes Hailey and Myla, but they have something fundamental in common. All three are Black athletes who perform to the best of their abilities every time they grab a rowing oar or a lacrosse stick.

They are some "of the few" who are silencing the noise that simply being a member of the team sometimes brings to the sports they love. And, in using the magic that emanates from them, they have given the next generation of young Black women athletes a fighting chance to feel the freedom to just play.

She Builds a Space for Women

TIMBER TINA AND LUMBERJACK SPORTS

By Erica Block

Tina Scheer purchased thirty-five acres of land in Maine, and she didn't tell anyone about it. It was 1995, she was thirty-five years old, and she had lived in Hayward, a timber-rich region in Wisconsin's remote Sawyer County, for her entire life. But the time had come to create a new home somewhere else. She wanted to run a lumberjack sports show of her own.

Tina's hometown is the capital of the lumberjack sports world. Every July since 1960, Hayward—population 2,579—balloons in size to host the annual Lumberjack World Championships.

If right now you're thinking, "What are lumberjack sports?" then you are not from Hayward. Growing up in the Northwoods region, like Tina did, means growing up surrounded by logging history. You would need to be living in a cocoon to come from Hayward and to not know *something* about log rolling, the underhand chop, or axe throwing. It would be like growing up in the South Bronx unaware of the New York Yankees or living in Park City and being unfamiliar with skiing.

The sport's origins go back to the Industrial Revolution, when the US economy relied on the thriving lumber industry. After World War II, the use of hand tools to harvest lumber began to wane in the United States, and the North American logging industry turned to machinery to handle the tasks once performed by lumberjacks. Logging sports pay homage to this preindustrial history. Using tools powered by their own muscles, logging-sports athletes face off in timed contests that employ techniques once used in forestry: the log roll, pole climb, axe throw, and a variety of wood-block chopping and sawing races.

The Lumberjack World Championships are a premiere event for the sport. Each July, the best lumberjack-sports athletes from around the world—not just North America but also Australia, New Zealand, and Western Europe—all travel to Tina's small Wisconsin town to compete.

When ABC began covering the Lumberjack World Championships for the network's *Wide World of Sports* program in the 1970s, a palpable excitement enveloped the town. "You would literally have your backyard on national television," Tina recalls. "It was a big deal."

Tina, the youngest of six, was seven years old when her father left the family. In the wake of his departure, Tina's mom signed the youngest four siblings up for log rolling lessons to keep them occupied during summer afternoons. Log rolling is a battle of balance, where two opponents attempt to outlast each other as they "run" on a rolling log that is floating in water.

Almost every day, the Scheer kids walked three miles to the facility where lessons took place to practice dueling against one another. Tina and her siblings became really, really good at it. They started staging little log rolling exhibitions in their hometown. Eventually, once they were in their late teens, Tina and her siblings put together a lumberjack entertainment act and began charging admission to their performances. Word of Scheer's Lumberjack Show spread throughout the community.

Recognizing the demand for this kind of entertainment at festivals and fairs across the country, the Scheer siblings took their lumberjack sports show on the road. They bought a truck and trailer, and for the next fifteen years, "Timber Tina" worked in her family's business as a performer in their lumberjack shows, which were run by her older brothers.

Tina began making a name for herself as a logging sports competitor and athlete, not merely an entertainer in her family's show. As a teen, she appeared on the CBS TV program *Challenge of the Sexes*, where she log-rolled against Fred Wickheim, the reigning Canadian champion. In 1985, Tina and her sawing partner, Jim Alexander, traveled to Australia, where they won the Jack & Jill (coed) crosscut-sawing event at the Melbourne

Royal Woodchop Championships. They won again in 1988, this time with an extra teammate: She and Alexander secured their first-place finish while Tina was pregnant with her son, Charlie. And in 1989, they won another Jack & Jill crosscut-sawing title—this time at the Lumberjack World Championships, back in Tina's hometown.

What Tina really wanted, though, was to compete against other women. She enjoyed Jack & Jill sawing events, but she didn't want to be a small, blonde novelty surrounded by bearded, burly lumberjacks. She just wanted to chop and saw against opponents subject to the same physiology

A young Tina Scheer log rolling

and biology as she was. But women's competitive divisions in most professional lumberjack events simply did not exist.

In our country's lore—whether we're telling the tale of Paul Bunyan or watching an old *Looney Tunes* cartoon—lumberjacks are the paradigm of rugged masculinity and physical strength. Lumberjacks, in short, are men.

Timbersports competitions feature several dozen different events and races, in a format similar to that of a track or swim meet. Over the course of a two- or three-day-long competition, Jack & Jill sawing races would be the only mixed-gender event.

Log rolling contests, perhaps because they aren't overtly strength-based and don't feature sharp tools, have long existed for women. Local newspapers in the United States and Canada show photos of women participating in log rolling "roleos" as early as the 1930s, and the Lumberjack World Championships has always featured women's log rolling events on the competition slate. But wood chopping and sawing? Using sharp, heavy equipment to destroy wood faster than the person next to you? That was an all-male pursuit.

Tina was determined to change that.

In 1993, Tina approached the board of the Lumberjack World Championships to propose adding a women's chopping and sawing division. Creating opportunities for women to compete was the right thing to do, *and* she knew there was demand for it, from both the women lumberjack athletes who wanted to compete and the potential audience who would pay money to watch. The board said no. She tried again the next year; again, the board turned her down.

But she persevered. "I've never been the kind of person to get mad at someone for not doing something that I wanted done. But I never stopped inching forward," she says. "I would just think, *Well, this is going to happen; it's just going to take a little longer.* Look at the suffragettes—they were thrown in jail and force-fed for what they were trying to do. I just have to keep edging away at these guys till it happens."

When it comes to carving out a place for women to compete and to have opportunities in logging sports, Tina maintains a kind of relentless tunnel vision. How fiercely determined does a person have to be to look at people like Elizabeth Cady Stanton or Lucretia Mott—arguably two of the most extraordinary Americans of the twentieth century—and think, *If they can achieve their goals for women, then I can too.*

Leading up to the 1995 Lumberjack World Championships, Tina approached the board for a third time.

We don't have enough time in the schedule to run women's events, they told her, again.

"We could do [the women's chopping and sawing] in the morning," Tina suggested.

We don't have the money, the board told her, again.

Tina was ready for them to say as much. "I'll get the money," she said.

We don't have enough judges and timers to run these events, the board told her, again.

Tina refused to accept their excuses. "I said, we'll get the guys to do it. We'll get the other lumberjacks to do it." The board had run out of reasons to say no. They finally said yes.

Tina, at long last, had convinced the board to integrate women's events into the Championships lineup. Now she needed to put her money where her mouth was.

Tina went straight to work. She single-handedly began raising the prize money needed for the winner's purse in the women's events. Friends, friends of friends, members of the Hayward community, and even a local candy shop contributed. Tina wrote letters to every female timbersports athlete she knew, inviting them to compete. She reached out to women on college lumberjack sports teams and traveled to their competitions to recruit them in person. (Although there were few professional women's timbersports, varsity and club-level teams at colleges and universities had long offered women's divisions.) It was imperative for the women to show up en masse. Women finally had a chance to compete in the Lumberjack World Championships. Now they had to prove that they wanted to be there.

Did Tina worry about failing to deliver, if not with the prize money, then on her promise to field enough women entrants? There was a lot at stake and a lot resting on her shoulders. But in moments when she started to feel the weight of it all, Tina found herself thinking one thought: *If I don't do this, who else will?*

At the 1995 Lumberjack World Championships, female competitors outnumbered male competitors. The public response to the women's competition was overwhelmingly positive. "It worked," Tina says. "We showed up." Her organizing efforts had paid off. And ever since then, the most prestigious lumberjack sports contest in the country has featured women competing against other women. "The women's events are just as popular as the men's now," Tina says, and the quality of the women's competition is the highest it's ever been.

Hayward's Lumberjack World Championships remained an outlier throughout the 1990s and into the twenty-first century. Other lumberjack sports competitions in North America have been slower to provide women with opportunities to compete against other women. From 1990 to 2004, Tina served as an announcer and color commentator for the Stihl Timbersports Series on ESPN. Yet even with Tina serving as the literal voice of their competitions, Stihl only began offering a separate contest division for women on its college circuit in 2008. Stihl moved even slower in adding a women's division to their professional circuit—which didn't happen until 2017. Carving out opportunities for women in lumberjack sports is an ongoing fight.

"It's been my whole life. Nothing but," Tina says, of promoting women in logging sports and promoting the sport as a whole. "I feel like I'm the little engine who never stops running." This is the core of Tina's identity. She says, "I can't tell you how many people I know in timbersports who see something isn't going right, but they don't do anything about it. You've got to sit down at your computer, write something out, make phone calls. That's how it gets done; you just keep forging ahead. You don't just sit home and wish that it happens—you have to go for it."

This ability to actualize what she wants to accomplish is what led Tina to buy thirty-five acres of land along Route 3 in Trenton, Maine. For fifteen years, she had been part of Scheer's Lumberjack Show, the family business run by her brother, and in that stretch she had tackled nearly every facet of the show: performing, announcing, driving the truck, handling administrative matters. She loved her family, but her brother kept

Tina found herself thinking one thought: If I don't do this, who else will?

promoting other men into the show's more lucrative management roles. Instead of growing resentful or accepting the status quo, Tina set out to develop her own lumberjack entertainment show.

"I thought, I'm not going to get my way here, so I'm going to go somewhere else. And I bought the property before I told [my brothers] I was leaving," Tina says. She set up a dinner meeting with her brothers to let them know about her plans.

On the day before the meeting, one of her brothers called. He wanted to chat with Tina one-on-one, before their group dinner with the whole crew. They met up over lunch.

"I want to offer you a management job in the show," her brother said.

Tina looked at him. "I just bought thirty-five acres of land in Maine, and I'm going to start my own lumberjack show," she said. "I quit."

Her brother congratulated her.

At her new property, Tina and her then-husband cleared nearly two acres of heavily wooded land and began building a site for the Great Maine Lumberjack Show. They constructed bleachers and erected giant wooden poles for speed climbing. The project-in-progress intrigued the local community. "Scheer plans to build a big pool about two to three feet deep, where log rollers will perform on an eleven-foot-long cedar log," the *Bangor Daily News* reported.

Getting the Great Maine Lumberjack Show off the ground wasn't so easy. The town rejected Tina's initial business plan and application for a land-use permit. She was an outsider in Maine. Members of the local community were intrigued, but they also remained skeptical about her plan to start a live lumberjack entertainment show. They hadn't heard of such a thing. "When a Wisconsin woman calling herself Timber Tina came to Maine last year planning to open the Great Maine Lumberjack Show, a few eyebrows were raised," a *Bangor Daily News* columnist wrote. "How could someone from away, even from a major logging state like Wisconsin, possibly showcase the skills for which Maine was once famous?"

Then there was the issue of the weather. The summer of 1996 in New England was particularly cold and rainy, and so the site construction on Tina's property was running behind schedule.

One of the first lumberjack performers Tina hired was Dave Smith, who now coaches Colby College's logging sports team in Waterville, Maine. Dave remembers checking out Tina's site in Trenton while it was still being built. "It was very much a work in progress. I went over there, and the place was just a mud pit. She was very frustrated with the whole process. Everything was moving along very slowly because the weather was miserable, and she was having trouble finding people who could do the work, and I think she didn't have as much money as she would have liked to get the whole thing started."

They were a couple of months behind schedule, but by the end of July, the construction of the necessary infrastructure was complete. The Great Maine Lumberjack Show debuted—and the cold, wet weather continued. It was a terrible season for Maine tourism all around. The show wasn't exactly an immediate success. "Word hadn't gotten around yet," Dave says. "If we got twenty or fifty people in the audience, we were kind of ecstatic. Somewhere along the way, we broke one hundred people and we were excited about that."

But, as always, Tina persevered. Word of Timber Tina's Great Maine Lumberjack Show gradually spread, and Tina and the show itself became part of the local community. She and her team of performers showcased their wood-chopping and sawing skills at local events like the Paul Bunyan Festival and Bar Harbor's Fourth of July parade, and as pregame entertainment before Bangor Blue Ox minor-league baseball games.

A turning point came in 1997, when Stihl selected Tina's property in Maine as a site for that year's Timbersports Series' regional qualifier contests. ESPN sent a crew and production truck to cover the event, providing valuable exposure. Millions of viewers tuned in when the pretaped competition aired later that year. Once again, Tina saw her backyard featured on national television.

Tina also began offering log rolling lessons in an effort to introduce a younger generation to the sport. Despite Maine's history and ties to the timber industry, many locals were unaware that logging had evolved into a competitive sport. The kids she encountered in the Northeast, unlike those in Hayward, didn't know about log rolling, the underhand chop, or crosscut sawing. Tina set out to change that. Her son, Charlie, was one of her best students.

In 2004, tragedy struck. Tina was accepted to compete in the TV show *Survivor: Guatemala*. But mere days before she was set to leave, Charlie died in an automobile accident. He was sixteen. "I wanted everyone to know about him," Tina wrote for Umission. "It is the only way I can keep him alive. His name was Charlie. He log rolled in the show with me. He chopped. He chain sawed. That's a hole that will never be filled."

Charlie loved watching *Survivor*, and before he died, Tina had sent CBS an audition tape to compete on the show. After being selected to participate, nobody was more excited for Tina than Charlie was. She decided not to leave for Guatemala while grieving him, but she proceeded to compete in the following season of *Survivor*, seeing through the plan she and Charlie had made together. Tina's outdoor skills landed her on another reality show in 2013, when she was the only woman to compete in the National Geographic Channel's wilderness reality show *Ultimate Survival: Alaska.*

In the offseason, when the stream of tourists visiting Maine tapers off, Tina takes her show on the road. Together with several women performers in her Great Maine Lumberjack Show, Tina formed the World Champion Lumberjills, also known as "Chics with Axes." This all-female tour crisscrosses the country, providing logging sports demonstrations at state fairs, heritage festivals, and other events. More than businesses or entertainment acts, the Great Maine Lumberjack Show and Tina's World Champion Lumberjills have served as channels to reestablish and grow the popularity of logging sports.

Tina also mentors the next generation of female logging athletes. Recently, Tina flew to Milwaukee to watch one of her Lumberjills, Samantha Graves, compete in the US Women's Championship. In the women's standing block chopping event, Graves beat the women's world record by just under one second. Graves had raised the bar for women's chopping— and she did it while wearing a Great Maine Lumberjack Show T-shirt.

They Keep Competing

WHEN AGE IS JUST A NUMBER

By Leila Sales, with reporting contributed by Erin Gee

There's no age that's necessarily "too old" for sports. My nearly eighty-year-old mother relishes going on long bike rides and hikes. On days that are too cold or snowy, you'll find her at the gym, lifting weights next to girls a third of her age. (She recently bought a matching sports bra and leggings set from Old Navy so she would "fit in" with her gym-going compatriots, though she says she still cannot figure out how they get their ponytails so bouncy.)

Even competitive sports can be enjoyed by people at any age. The United States Adult Soccer Association hosts an annual tournament for teams of women all over the age of seventy, and from what I hear, it's viciously competitive.

But athletes at the very top levels? Olympians, professionals, world champions? Those people tend to be young.

Many female athletes who make it to the elite level retire from there in their twenties. It makes sense: What they do is incredibly hard on their bodies. At the Tokyo Olympics, the average ages for female gymnasts and swimmers were twenty-one and twenty-two, respectively. This is young, but it's actually older than it used to be—2021 was the first Olympics since

1968 where teen gymnasts were outnumbered by non-teens. At the 2012 Olympics, 99 percent of the athletes were under the age of forty.

Knowing these statistics is what makes you realize how remarkable Oksana Chusovitina is.

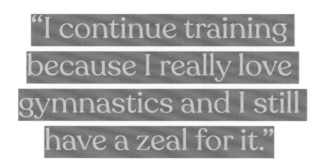

"I continue training because I really love gymnastics and I still have a zeal for it."

Chusovitina, an Uzbekistani gymnast, has competed at eight Olympic Games. The first was in 1992, at the age of seventeen; the most recent was in 2021, at the age of forty-six. Only three of the ninety-six other women up against Chusovitina in Tokyo were even *alive* when she first arrived on the world stage.

Over the course of those three decades, she has competed under three different flags, given birth to a son, and won more than thirty medals at international meets.

A career of such longevity is remarkable in any field, but especially in one that's so physically demanding. The flipping, twisting, and arching required by the sport come with a high risk of injury—if not a dramatic one caused by, say, misjudging your distance from the end of a balance beam during a dismount, then a more mundane repetitive-use injury or stress fracture caused by thousands of hard landings.

How has Chusovitina managed to stay competitive at an elite level for so long? She's credited both her genes and her perseverance—and surely luck in avoiding a career-ending injury has played a role too—but ultimately, she admitted, "I can't answer that question. I don't know." She claimed (though, as an observer, I find this extremely hard to believe) that she's "an ordinary person. . . . Nothing phenomenal about me, just stuck in sports a little longer." The secret to her longevity? She's joked, "When I retire from the sport, I will definitely tell you what the secret is."

Perhaps the secret is the joy she takes in doing it. "I continue training because I really love gymnastics and I still have a zeal for it" she told *International Gymnast* at the age of thirty-three, when she was already being interviewed about how old she was. More than a decade later, she's giving the same answer: "It doesn't matter how old you are; it matters what you do," she told *USA Today*. "I just do it because this is what I love. And I always say if you do something, put your soul and your heart into it." In short, she's said, "As long as I am able to do this, as long as I like it, I will continue doing it."

While Chusovitina's love for the sport hasn't changed with age, her training regimen has. She no longer does as many repetitions of her routines as she once did; it's tough on her body, and she doesn't need it. By now, the moves are fully part of her.

Chellsie Memmel, another older elite gymnast, has also spoken about the need to change her approach to training. When Memmel represented the United States at the 2008 Olympics, she was twenty years old and she trained constantly, even when injured. After a long hiatus, during which time she had two children, she returned to elite competition at the age of thirty-two. She paces herself differently this time around. She's said she does gymnastics only three days a week and rarely does any given move more than five times in a single training session. (Three days a week doesn't feel like an "only" to me, but for an elite athlete, that shows remarkable moderation.) At her age, "it's keeping those numbers low and just focusing on quality," Memmel said.

Diver Laura Wilkinson, who won gold at age twenty-two at the 2000 Olympics and then staged a comeback twenty years later, has said the same thing. "Training now is about quality of workouts rather than quantity of dives. . . . It's refreshing to be a part of this again, and I still have passion for it. It's a part of my life again, but it's not my whole life anymore."

Another pool-based superstar, swimmer Dara Torres, medaled at five Olympics. The first was when she was seventeen; the most recent was when she was forty-one. In 2008, she was the oldest swimmer to win a medal in Olympic history. Some people were so stunned by this accomplishment that they accused her of doping. She wasn't, and she thought they were ridiculous for doubting her. "If Nolan Ryan could pitch a no-hitter at forty-four years old, and Jack Nicklaus can win a Masters at forty-six, why couldn't a forty-one-year-old mom make an Olympic team?" Torres said to *People*. "Why was there such a stigma against a woman doing that after having a kid?"

Like Memmel and Wilkinson, Torres's training regimen changed with age. "You have to listen to your body," she said. Her perspective changed too. It's not that she became less competitive but that she was more willing to show herself grace. She describes a race that she lost by one-one hundredth of a second. "I thought I would never be able to let that go. But what I did as I got older was to look back and ask myself, 'Did I really do everything I could have, to be the best I could be?' Overall I was able to see that I *did* do my best. That comes with general maturity."

This sort of shifting mentality is just as important for older athletes as shifting their training. Now forty-eight, Chusovitina feels liberated by having nothing left to prove. "I am at such an age and in such a position that I do this for myself", and I'm very interested in proving to myself whether I can do it or not," she told *International Gymnast* in 2023. "Therefore, I will try so as not to regret it later."

When asked how she feels about competing against and alongside gymnasts who are much younger than her, Chusovitina told *International*

"I am at such an age and in such a position that I do this for myself."

Gymnast, "I think it's good that they will see that I am still competing. They will think it's normal to continue on." Other gymnasts look up to her, but they also take her seriously as a competitor. "We're all equal on the field of play," she told Olympics.com. "I have never felt uncomfortable in any way. I've never felt that the girls look at me like, oops, I'm so old and performing. Never."

Like gymnastics, figure skating is a sport known for its lithe young athletes. Six of the seven most recent Olympic champions in women's singles figure skating have been under the age of twenty-one. Deanna Stellato-Dudek was one such young athlete. At sixteen, she won a silver medal at the 2000 World Junior Championships. But soon after her senior international debut, she sustained a series of hip injuries and retired from competition.

But she couldn't stay away forever. After a long hiatus, during which time she worked as an aesthetician in Chicago, Stellato-Dudek returned to the rink, this time in pairs skating. In 2024, she became the oldest female figure skater to win a world title. She was forty years old.

"If I could talk to my younger self, I think my younger self would think I'm crazy," Stellato-Dudek said. "She wanted to win the 2006 Olympics, so she would be wondering why I'm going for the 2026 Olympics."

Like Chusovitina, Stellato-Dudek recognizes the influence her perseverance can have on the next generation of athletes. "I hope a lot of athletes stay around a lot longer. I hope it encourages people to not stop before they reach their potential, and I hope it transcends into other areas, not just in sports, but also in other areas of life, like work and professional careers."

We can't talk about women on the ice without talking about Hayley Wickenheiser. She played on Canada's national hockey team for twenty-three years, retiring in 2017 at the age of thirty-eight. In that time, she competed at the Olympics six times, playing hockey at five Winter Olympics and softball at one Summer Olympics. (Hey, if you're amazing at one sport, why *not* be amazing at two?)

As the years passed, what started to bother Wickenheiser wasn't her age so much as outsiders' fascination with it. "You feel the age comment start to come up, and I didn't like it. . . . When I finished my last Olympics in Sochi [at age thirty-five], I was tied for the most points and played thirty-six minutes, the most minutes out of any player on the team in the gold medal final. So, for me, age is just a number."

Another Canadian icon is Christine Sinclair, who played on Canada's national soccer team from 2000 to 2023 before retiring at the age of forty. She competed at four Olympics, beat the world record (for men *and* women) for most international goals scored (190 total!), and made 331 senior appearances. At the 2019 World Cup, Sinclair's coach described her as "potentially the fittest you've ever seen her"—despite her being thirty-six at the time, a decade older than the average age of the other players on the field. At the 2023 World Cup, her last before retiring, she was the second-oldest competitor.

How do you know when it's time to retire? The athletes who get to ask that question, who get to make that choice for themselves rather than being forced out by injury or other circumstances beyond their control—they are the fortunate ones. But it's so hard to leave when you've given your life to a sport. "I guess there's no right time," Wickenheiser told

Sportsnet on the occasion of her own retirement. "I'll miss the game. I'll miss going to the rink. . . . I'll miss practicing, I'll miss training, I'll miss playing." But, she said, "there were things in my life I just really didn't want to wait for anymore. . . . It's very emotional, because it's something you've loved your whole life."

Hanging it up isn't easy—and, as athletes like Memmel, Wilkinson, and Stellato-Dudek have shown, a goodbye doesn't always last forever. Within months of retiring from the Canadian national soccer team, Sinclair had re-signed with her club team, the Portland Thorns. Her international career might be behind her, but her days of professional soccer playing surely are not.

"It's impossible to be fully ready for ending your career," Chusovitina said. Though she has announced her retirement from gymnastics at least twice, it hasn't stuck yet. She joked, "We are women; we are so fickle. Today, we say yes; tomorrow, we say no. I just realized, I felt that I can do this. Why should I leave the sport if it brings me joy?"

> "Why should I leave the sport if it brings me joy?"

"PEOPLE
BELIEVED IN ME,
I BELIEVED
IN MYSELF,
AND HERE I AM.
SO, IF I CAN
DO IT,
SO CAN YOU."

Caitlin Clark

She Says Watch Me Do It

ALIA ISSA TAKES ON THE WORLD

By Safaa Sallal in collaboration with Egab

"In my first international tournament, I was very nervous," twenty-three-year-old Alia Issa recalls, with the kind of smile that could disarm skeptics and inspire motivational posters. "But then I thought, *Be strong; you've got this.*"

This wasn't just a pep talk. It was a declaration of war against the odds.

In 2021, Alia Issa, a Greek national of Syrian decent, became the first female parathlete to represent refugees on an Olympic stage. She competed in the Tokyo Paralympics as part of the second-ever Refugee Paralympic Team. As one of the team's six athletes—three from Syria, one from Iran, one from Afghanistan, and one from Burundi—Alia helped represent the estimated 110 million displaced people around the world.

Alia was born in 2001 to Syrian refugees who had sought asylum in Greece. Her fourth birthday was less about cake and candles and more about a life-or-death battle with chicken pox, which caused motor neuropathy and other complications in her central nervous system, leaving her with a physical disability and a silenced voice. But here's the thing about Alia: When life handed her lemons, she didn't just make lemonade—she started a lemonade empire.

"I am not a person with special needs," she says. "I'm a person with superpowers."

After years of physiotherapy, speech therapy, and medical treatments, Alia reclaimed her mobility and voice, not only to speak but to roar. At the age of eight, she was finally able to leave her bed. Despite being bound to a wheelchair, she felt that simply being able to move and speak was a miracle.

Alia recalls the bullying she endured when she started school. She remembers the classmates who taunted her, who pushed her away every time she tried to get close.

"Why do you stutter?" they would ask.

"You belong at home, not in school!"

"Don't be friends with her or else you'll turn out like her."

The words were meant to hurt, and they did.

"During my first week at school, I used to wish the earth would open up and swallow me," Alia says. "I couldn't bear the teasing, mocking, and bullying. In my mind, I was just like them but I had a special health condition. But this was something other kids didn't understand or accept."

Alia took matters into her own hands. She made a conscious decision to ignore the bullying and arm herself with hope and perseverance. She set a goal for herself: *I will show them who Alia is and what she is capable of.*

The bullies tried to clip her wings, but Alia was already in flight. "An ear made of clay and the other made of dough," she quips, using a Syrian saying to describe turning a deaf ear to haters while shaping her destiny with the other.

After elementary, Alia moved to a special needs school. That was the first spark that created a champion out of a victim, she says. "I molded the discrimination and bullying into motivation that pushed me forward instead of holding me back," she says.

"I am not a person with special needs. I'm a person with superpowers."

One spring day in 2017, sixteen-year-old Alia witnessed a scene that changed everything. She saw other people with mobility limitations playing sports, and a fire was ignited within her.

"*Why don't I try?* I thought to myself," she recalls, a bright twinkle in her eyes. "What's the worst that could happen? I fail? At least I tried."

After tryouts for various sports, including cycling and boccia, Alia found herself drawn to the club throw, in which athletes compete to throw a wooden club as far as possible. The club throw is one of four Paralympic throwing events; the others are discus, javelin, and shot put.

Although Alia was young for club throwing, the strength of her arms was obvious, and she displayed a tremendous talent and power.

Greek parathletes coach Dionisis Koubaris remembers that the first time Alia tried the club throw, she achieved seven meters. But she kept at it, throwing greater and greater distances, until only six months later she reached 15 meters, then 20.

"At the beginning of her training, Alia had issues with balance," Dionisis says. "We worked together to improve that through continuous exercises and hard work." Alia committed herself to training two hours at least every day after school, even if she was tired. That daily routine became part of her.

Dionisis describes Alia as a flame of energy that doesn't wane. "Alia is a very special girl, and this is what I noticed when I saw her train with the team," he says. Cheerful and loved by all team members, says Dionisis, Alia's constant smile even when they are facing difficulties always keeps her teammates going.

"Club throwing needs a lot of strength and determination," Alia says. "And I used to draw that strength from my mother, who has never been embarrassed of me."

Indeed, when Fatima Al-Najjar, Alia's mother, talks about her daughter, she is full of pride and admiration.

"I have never been ashamed of my daughter," she says. "On the contrary, I am proud of her. I believe in her. She is capable and determined. I will confront any community that rejects her, even relatives who live miles away in Syria."

Fatima says that some families who have children with special needs are ashamed of them and choose to lock themselves and their children in their homes to avoid going out and being seen in public with them.

"I am not like that. I held my daughter's hand and took her everywhere. We heard whispers and comments, but I met every sentence with a smile and told Alia, 'It's okay, everything is going to be okay; I am proud to be your mother,'" she says.

When Alia's father passed away in 2016, Fatima became the sole parent for Alia and her five siblings. It was a lot of responsibility, especially since many of their family members remain in Syria.

"I endured many hardships. Everyone kept telling me, 'Don't waste your energy on Alia; just accept her condition and focus your attention on her siblings.' But I wasn't fazed by their words. I didn't even bother to react to them.

"I have raised her bit by bit, and my faith in her and in God is great," she says.

And like her daughter, Fatima resorts to popular sayings to summarize what she and her family have gone through: What doesn't break you makes you stronger.

"The first challenge was Alia's illness, the second was my husband's death from cancer, and the third was my eldest daughter getting cancer. But whatever we went through made me stronger, more patient, and more determined," she says.

Alia finds a perfect popular saying to describe the inspiration she draws from her mother: "Turn the pot upside down, the girl will be like her mother." She adds, "I am like my mother—very strong, and I never give up. She is my source of inspiration and strength. She cheers me on whenever I compete. I win for her and in honor of my father's memory," she says.

Since taking up club throwing, Alia has competed in tournaments all over the world, from Switzerland to Athens, Bologna, and Thessaloniki. She is now able to walk, but she doesn't have full range of movement, and sometimes she shakes. She uses a wheelchair mainly to get around but not when she's competing.

"The moment I throw the club, I feel like I have the wings of a bird longing to fly, that I am free, strong, happy, and triumphant over everyone who betted on my failure and bullied me. I am triumphant over myself and my illness," she says.

Alia made history when she qualified for the Tokyo Paralympics. It was only the second time that a Refugee Team competed at the Summer Paralympics, and Alia was both the youngest and the only woman on the team.

As she carried the flag at the opening ceremony, she felt she was carrying refugees' dreams of returning to their homelands across the world. "All I was thinking was that one day, I will represent my own country and carry my own flag," she says.

According to the United Nations, of the 110 million people forcibly displaced worldwide, at least 12 million of them have special needs.

"Our participation was an exceptional experience in my athletic career, and I want it to be an inspiring experience for all persons with disabilities," Alia says. Her message to female athletes and parathletes everywhere? "Don't give up, and don't give in to society's prejudice and bullying. Stand up with all the power God gave you."

Dionisis has a photo of himself with Alia during the Tokyo Olympics, and he describes that moment as one of the happiest of his life. "I will frame and hang this photo in my house so I can see it every day. It inspires optimism and determination in moments when I am not okay," he says.

"To know a person for who they truly are, you need to get closer to them and not judge them based on appearances," he says. "They might blow you away with their skills and capabilities, and they [might] teach you more than you can ever teach them."

As she looks toward the next Olympics and her dreams of pursuing a degree in oncology, one thing is clear: Alia Issa isn't just a Paralympic athlete. She's a force of nature, a warrior with a smile, and a woman who dresses not in the expectations of others but in the strength and determination that are uniquely her own.

"I want to win medals for my homeland, Syria; my family; and everyone who believed in me," Alia says. "With strength and determination, what I wish for is an inevitable reality."

They Aren't Intimidated

THE MAYAN REBELS

By Erica Block

Mayan women living in rural communities along Mexico's Yucatán Peninsula typically lead fairly isolated lives. Even as women in other parts of Mexico have made economic and social gains, Mayan women in the Yucatán face a number of obstacles when it comes to pursuing an education or career. Gender roles are traditional and circumscribed, and women are discouraged from having hobbies or social lives outside their household and family. In these small rural communities, girls tend to see their lives shrink, rather than expand, as they become women.

Growing up in Yaxuná, a town in the heart of the state of Yucatán, Maria Enedina Canul Poot occasionally snuck out of her house to play games and sports with other kids at a nearby field. The fifty-four-year-old remembers how satisfying it felt to subvert the boys' expectations of her by proving she could play. "I was the only seven-year-old girl in the village who could give them a good game," she explained to *Mexico News Daily* reporter Mark Viales in 2023. Canul Poot took pride in holding her own.

Persuading her mom to let her go outside and play with the boys wasn't easy. "I would argue with her to allow me to play, even though she beat me, but I would do everything possible to convince her to let me go and play," Canul Poot told Viales. "Eventually, she relented."

When Canul Poot reached her early teens, her mom's insistence that she act more feminine became harder to challenge. Eventually, Canul Poot's mother gave Canul Poot an ultimatum: She could either give up playing pickup games outside or risk being thrown out of her family's house.

It's a depressing image: a young, adventurous girl glimpsing the narrow limits of her future. Her life wasn't supposed to include fun. Canul Poot had grown up listening to Yucatán Lions games on the radio and watching men in the community play baseball. But as a woman, she wasn't supposed to pursue this sport she loved.

Fermina Antonia Dzib Dzul grew up in Yaxcabá, another small Mayan community on the Yucatán Peninsula. Growing up in Yaxcabá, Dzib Dzul, who's now forty-four, loved running around outdoors and playing with other kids in the neighborhood. But her mother often forbade Dzib Dzul from playing outside and generally disapproved of her venturing off alone beyond their family's house by herself. Dzib Dzul hated that she had to choose between obeying her mother and playing outside.

Canul Poot's and Dzib Dzul's stories of their mothers discouraging them from participating in sports—and even just recreational play—reflect the sexist attitudes that are deeply ingrained in their Mayan communities. Traditionally, their culture has placed hard limits on what the lives of women can look like. But more recently, those limits have begun to loosen, thanks to a surprising development. Softball, of all things, has become an unexpected source of empowerment and liberation for Mayan women in the Yucatán, empowering them to challenge their status quo and live fuller, less restricted lives.

It all started back in 2017, when public health officials working for Mexico's Ministry for Social Development (SEDESOL) set up a fitness program in Yaxuná as part of a wellness initiative to combat rising rates of diabetes and hypertension among women in Yucatán state. Canul Poot, whose doctor had recently recommended that she exercise more, was among a dozen or so women participating in the program in Yaxuná. Initially, the government officials proposed aerobics as a cardiovascular activity for the women. Inspired by her childhood interests, Canul Poot suggested a different idea to the group: Why not play softball?

"I'm a sportswoman, so dancing and jumping around just doesn't do it for me," Canul Poot told Viales. "I prefer the atmosphere and camaraderie of competitive team sports. . . . Baseball is the sport of Yucatán and the game I fell in love with from a young age."

Canul Poot's suggestion resonated with other women participating in the fitness program, and softball became a source of both fitness and camaraderie for women of all ages in the community.

At first, their equipment was makeshift: The women played pickup games with a handmade bat that Canul Poot had carved herself. Sometime later, a local baseball team donated equipment for the women to use, and soon the informal, modified ball game they had been playing several afternoons a week evolved into organized softball practices and scrimmages to refine their skills.

The women's passion for the game kept growing, and, no longer under the guise of a sanctioned public health program, their decision to continue playing softball became an act of defiance. The women ballplayers in Yaxuná chose to call themselves "Las Amazonas," in homage to the female warriors of Greek mythology who were defined by their physical agility, strength, and endurance. "This is what I felt we were: women warriors. I could definitely identify with this name, and I am delighted it stuck," Canul Poot said to Viales.

Meanwhile, about 130 kilometers east of Yaxuná, in the small village of Hondzonot, a group of women who had participated in the same public health initiative as the Amazonas formed a softball team too. The women in Hondzonot decided to call themselves "Las Diablillas" (the Little Devils). They chose the name because they know that their playing softball is inherently a rebellious act.

When the Diablillas or the Amazonas take the field, their aesthetic on the diamond is distinct. Both teams play and practice wearing their chosen uniform: bright-white huipils, which are traditional Mesoamerican garments trimmed with colorful embroidery. Notably, the women prefer to play barefoot, without cleats or shoes.

The Amazonas' unusual and visually distinct uniforms stood out when, in 2019, a tourist exploring the Yucatán recorded a video of Canul Poot hitting a home run. In the video, Canul Poot holds up the skirt of her huipil as she runs around the bases. The home run went viral. The Mayan women who play softball barefoot and compete in huipils gained national and international media attention. No longer unknown, the Amazonas and the Diablillas began to forge connections in the international-sports landscape. They've also inspired women in nearby communities to form their own teams, says Flor Liliana Moo Keb, who plays shortstop for the Amazonas.

"We have seen many towns and villages produce double the number of all-female teams they originally had," Moo Keb told Viales in a 2023 interview for the *Guardian*. "Perhaps softball can now be considered the state sport for women in Yucatán."

While the Diablillas and Amazonas still struggle with resources to finance travel to competitions and improvements to their practice field, they've gained more material support as the teams' notoriety grows. Coverage of Las Diablillas in outlets like the *New York Times* and Meadowlark Media's *Sports Explains the World* documentary series in the last few years have put these women softball players—and the way they are challenging deeply ingrained gender roles in their Mayan communities— on the global map.

In one example of their reach, Stefanía Aradillas, a member of the Mexican Olympic women's softball team and the 2020 National Sports Award winner, visited Hondzonot in 2021 to play a game with the Diablillas. Alejandra Tuz May, the Diablillas' nineteen-year-old catcher, said she wants to follow in Aradillas's footsteps.

Tuz May's goal is not out of reach. Women's softball in Yucatán continues to grow in the wake of teams like the Diablillas and the Amazonas garnering attention in news stories and on social media. At the college level, the Autonomous University of Yucatán (UADY) now has a women's softball team called the Jaguarcitas. And professional opportunities for women to play softball in Mexico are possible, too, with the Mexican Softball League (LMS) kicking off its inaugural season in 2024.

"[Aradillas's] story really touched me," Tuz May told the *Birmingham Times*' Julio Guzmán. "When she was young, she was discriminated against for being a woman in a league, and they wouldn't let her play, even though she was very good."

Not too long ago, a number of players on the Amazonas and Diablillas had never traveled outside their home village or flown on an airplane. But being part of a team and competing as athletes have helped the women on the Diablillas and Amazonas expand their identities beyond the domestic sphere of their households. By playing softball while outwardly expressing pride in their Mayan identity, the women are broadening the possibilities that their daughters and other young Mayan girls can envision when they contemplate their futures.

In July 2022, the Amazonas made history when they participated in the first all-female game to be played in a Mexican Baseball League (LMB) stadium. The game, promoted by the Yucatán government, took place at Kukulcán Alamo Stadium, the Yucatán Lions' home ballpark. Later that year, in a testament to the way the Amazonas have forged connections in the international-sports landscape, a group of Denver Broncos cheerleaders traveled to Yucatán state to play a friendly ball game against the Amazonas. The cheerleaders' trip was part of a program spearheaded by the NFL to drum up further interest in American football in Mexico.

Both teams have forged connections in American pro sports too.

Manuel Rodriguez, a relief pitcher in MLB's Chicago Cubs organization, is the first-ever Mexican player from Yucatán to play in the big leagues. Toward the end of the 2022 MLB season, the Diablillas sent Rodriguez a special gift to represent and celebrate their shared culture. Juana Ay Ay, the captain of the Diablillas, designed and embroidered a Chicago Cubs jersey with Yucatecan designs, the same ones that typically adorn their huipils. In a video posted to Facebook, Rodriguez unboxed the jersey and was visibly moved by the Diablillas' gift and message to him. Rodriguez said the embroidery reminded him of the designs his mom used to stitch into huipils for his sisters. This small example demonstrates the powerful ability of sport to connect people in disparate parts of the world.

Roughly a year after the Diablillas connected with Rodriguez, the Amazonas were invited to play an exhibition game at a major-league ball-park as part of programming for Hispanic Heritage Month: Chase Field, the Arizona Diamondbacks' home stadium in Phoenix. All this would have been unthinkable as recently as 2017, when the women first began playing. Not only has softball created a sense of community for the women, but it's also opened up a whole world of travel, competition, and diplomatic experiences.

The sports-retail business has taken notice of the Mayan women ball-players too. In September 2023, Champion Athleticwear chose to feature Las Diablillas as part of the company's new global brand campaign, "Champion What Moves You." It might not seem like a lot, but Champion is a multi-billion-dollar brand that has outfitted dozens of Olympic athletes and professional teams. Their desire to partner with the Diablillas is a big deal.

But however thrilling it is to partner with a brand like Champion, or to play in a real major-league stadium in the United States, the most essential thing that softball has provided the women is a sense of identity. Playing softball provides members of the Diablillas and Amazonas with another dimension of existence. In rural Mayan communities along the Yucatán Peninsula, women typically need to ask a man—usually their husband or father—for permission in order to leave the house or venture off into public spaces. Alicia Canul Dzib, who plays second base and pitches for Las Diablillas, says playing softball on this team has literally made her world bigger.

"I used to really only leave the house to help my husband with our crops," Canul Dzib said in a 2021 interview with Viales for the *New York Times*. "Now, thanks to softball, I have permission to leave the house, enjoy myself with friends, and visit new towns. It motivates me to keep playing and set an example for my daughter."

Softball has bestowed players on the Diablillas and Amazonas with the agency to experience new places and people. Being part of a team enables the women to be less homebound, and to develop a dynamic identity on top of being a wife and mother. For a number of the players, being an athlete has become an essential piece of their self-concept. The way a number of the women players present on social media illustrates this point.

Most of the women use a softball-related photo as their Facebook or Instagram profile picture—often a shot of game action or an image with teammates in their huipil uniforms.

> "Now, thanks to softball, I have permission to leave the house, enjoy myself with friends, and visit new towns. It motivates me to keep playing and set an example for my daughter."

On her Facebook page, the Diablillas' Tuz May proudly lists "softbolista" and "catcher #1" in her intro. She categorizes herself as an athlete and includes the quote, "No te dejes intimidar por un poco de poder (Don't be intimidated by a little power)" in the "About" section of her profile. The Amazonas' Thalia Poot Dzib features a candid shot of her pitching, mid-delivery, on her profile. In Spanish, the caption occupying the image reads, "The best version of me." In another section of Poot Dzib's profile, she says, "Mi pasión es el softbol," and she also gives a shout-out to her teammates on the Amazonas de Yaxunah.

Nearly all the women on both teams maintain social profiles like this, with photos and quotes that emphasize their identity as a ballplayer and athlete.

Before listing basic information like her location or gender, Fermina Dzib Dzul proudly claims, "Soy la capitana de las Auténticas y Verdaderas Amazonas de Yaxunah (I am the captain of the real and true Amazonas of Yaxunah)" on her Instagram profile. And the Diablillas' left fielder Geimi May uses one of her profiles to articulate the lessons she's learned from softball and how playing the sport has enhanced her life:

> *I invest in learning how to work with others and be a good teammate. I invest to learn to deal with disappointment when I don't get what I expected . . . I invest in learning to achieve my goals. I invest to understand that success doesn't happen overnight.*

The women on the Diablillas and Amazonas range in age from fourteen to sixty-four; many of them are wives and mothers, and some work as herders or seamstresses. But they all can add "ballplayer" to their multifaceted identities. Being an athlete and a woman were once mutually exclusive in Yucatán communities. Now the Amazonas and Diablillas have shown how the two are a perfect—and powerful—match.

They Defy Expectations

SAIL LIKE A GIRL

By Kylie Mohr

The ocean off western Canada was inky black when a small sailboat carrying seven women violently crashed into something. Those asleep jolted awake. It was the middle of the night, far from the lights of civilization, and electronic maps showed no rocks or land in the boat's path. *What on earth had they hit?*

Women scrambled up and around the boat with flashlights to check for damage. And there, bobbing in the water, was the culprit: a massive 30-foot log, 18 inches thick and wedged firmly underneath the bottom of the boat.

An errant log is just one of hundreds of things that can go wrong during the Race to Alaska, a 750-mile haul from Port Townsend, Washington, to Ketchikan, Alaska. It's a long race in remote waters, and here's the catch: Motors aren't allowed. Participants must race harnessing only their arms, legs, and the fickle wind. For good measure, no support crews are allowed either. The race's website dramatically likens the course to "the Iditarod, on a boat, with a chance of drowning, being run down by a freighter, or eaten by a grizzly bear." First place gets $10,000 in cash; second place gets a set of steak knives. Everyone else walks away empty-handed.

187

Meet the women who think that sounds fun: Jeanne Goussev, Anna Stevens, Haley King Lhamon, Allison Ekberg Dvaladze, Aimee Fulwell, Kate Hearsey McKay, Kelly Danielson, and Morgana Buell. A little too much orange whiskey had led them to that boat, in the middle of nowhere, in the summer of 2018.

It all started when Jeanne and her friend Anna were nursing a few drinks after a sailing race at the Cap Sante Marina in Anacortes, Washington, during the fall of 2017. Jeanne was fed up with the bro-y air that permeates yacht club parties. Sailing is a heavily male-dominated sport; in the Pacific Northwest, only about 5 percent of skippers (the leaders of a sailing crew) are women, according to Jeanne. She judges gender equality in the sport by the bathrooms at races, where lines typically snake out of the men's bathroom. But the women's room? She can breeze right in.

On this evening, she just couldn't take any more men strutting around, puffing out their chests, and bragging. So she fled to her boat, *Gray Wolf*, with her husband and a few close friends, including Anna and Morgana. That was when Anna blurted out the idea of forming an all-women's team for the Race to Alaska, an event she'd been flirting with joining for years. Jeanne and Morgana were all in. Jeanne was hungry for a challenge outside the daily grind. "I don't know who I am anymore," she remembered thinking. "I'm a mother, I'm an attorney, but that's not who I am. How do I go find my core again?" She felt a need to prove to herself that she could race on her own, without her husband. And thus, Team Sail Like a Girl was born.

First, Jeanne and her family bought a sailboat in California and drove it all the way back to their home on Bainbridge Island, Washington. Teammates, friends, and family stripped "her"—sailors always refer to boats with feminine pronouns—down to her studs and rebuilt her from scratch in Jeanne's barn-turned-sailyard. The boat, a style intended to sail short day races, needed upgrades for the voyage ahead. "We had to convert this Ferrari into a Humvee and make it something that was sustainable for a long period of time," Aimee said. An open-backed design was ideal for the human-powered piece of their strategy, which included two stationary bikes connected to rudders for propulsion. They would sail, and pedal, their way to Alaska.

A team of eight women in their thirties and forties slowly formed; seven sailed the majority of the voyage. Some were newbies; others, experts.

Aimee had grown up around water—swimming constantly as a child in Hawaii, rowing at the University of Washington in college. But she'd never sailed before coming aboard practice runs for the Race to Alaska. "I'm all about challenges," Aimee said. "The things that put me the most at ease mentally are moving meditations rather than something where I'm sitting still." Sailing felt like a natural fit.

But not everyone was supportive of the team. The women approached potential sponsors to help defray race costs and were met with skepticism. "We had a lot of naysayers leading up to it," Aimee said. "Whether it was sponsors or just people in general, thinking we were dumb for doing this." A local female sailor wrote the team an email prior to the race, saying they weren't fully thinking through all the risks. Others questioned if Jeanne, a mother, really understood she could die. *Do dads get these questions?* she wondered.

But the Sail Like a Girl teammates weren't deterred. At 5 a.m. on June 14, 2018, the team set off from the starting line in Port Townsend. Their goal wasn't to win. "I've always looked at this race as an adventure, and mainly, the goal is to survive," Anna said. Teams must reach Victoria, British Columbia, within a day and a half to qualify for the longest segment of the race, inside the Northwest Passage. Team Sail Like a Girl breezed their way to Canada.

Then, the real fun began. The leg from Victoria starts fast, with participants running down the docks and hopping on their boats. Then, it turns painfully slow, as teams can't hoist their sails until they've left the harbor and can only hope to catch the wind. The route they follow from there boasts incredibly variable conditions—choppy oceans or frustratingly calm waters that make moving without a motor almost impossible. Fog shrouds hazards like unmarked fishing vessels, and the most remote stretches of the race are multiple fuel refills of a Coast Guard helicopter away from any help.

After poking their way around a few islands, the team sailed down the Campbell River, an experience more akin to whitewater rafting than sailing. The first real crux of the route came at Seymour Narrows, a skinny stretch known for strong tidal currents. The water here is alive, churning and whirling with a mind of its own. Boaters must time their entrance and exit from the narrows just right or tides will sweep them backward, and a giant rock in the center only adds to the adrenaline rush. Sail Like a Girl got through the passage smoothly, sailing through without losing precious hours—or people.

The crew celebrated with cookies, baked and gifted to them by women who'd raced on coed teams in years past. The cookies were packed in a lunchbox along with a stack of index cards full of messages from women all around the world and inspirational quotes.

When the cookies were done, their journey north continued. Calm seas and minimal wind transformed the back of the boat into what felt like a never-ending spin class as women rotated between the bikes. Sometimes they sang to pass the time.

Near the end of Johnstone Strait, the wind suddenly whipped up. The women went from biking and singing to frantically trying to get away from a rocky shoreline they could've easily been tossed up on. Their boat went from almost no forward progress to a buckling 35 to 40 knots, or over 40 miles per hour. "Everything was going to hell in a handbasket," Aimee said. Some women had never been on a sailboat going that fast. Anna tried to take a sail down to slow the boat. Each time the boat hit a wave and got knocked sideways, her face dangled mere feet from the water. The wind eventually died down, and the team kept heading north.

Cruising past the halfway point at the Canadian village of Bella Bella, Team Sail Like a Girl had no clue where they stood among the other boats. They'd been without cell service for over twenty-four hours when their phones started exploding with texts and Facebook notifications. They were no longer in the dark—and they were currently in first place!

Suddenly, what started as a fun race with a group of women became something more. "All these women and all these little girls are following us, all over the world," Anna said. "Now we can't lose." Tensions on the boat ran high as cameras trained on the vessel and the women felt new-found pressure. A yoga instructor teammate, Kelly, led the crew in some calming breathing exercises to settle their nerves. The women sailed on— soon greeted by a pod of more than ten jumping, surfing orcas that played alongside their boat.

The sailboat continued its northward progress up Canada's rugged coastline, where heavily timbered mountains slouched downward to the ocean. The voyage was no five-star cruise: The crew was jammed into the 32-foot-long white boat like sardines. Quarters were so cramped that changing wet socks took close to forty-five minutes, said Jeanne, who

Team Sail Like a Girl

timed herself for fun. The women peed in buckets or, sometimes, rigged overboard. Beds consisted of yoga mats, shoved against the wall of the chilly fiberglass hull, and sleeping bags meant for o degrees Fahrenheit. Still, the cold water and cold air seeped into their bones. Salt clung to their skin, cracking and drying it out. "There's something really human that comes out when you walk away from the grunt of your everyday life, and you are tired and hungry and you've been working your butt off for hours and hours and days and days," Jeanne said.

By the time the team reached the large, undeveloped Aristazabal Island, the women were tired. Gusts of wind had buffeted them on and off for days. So they decided to take a calmer, smoother route on the inside of the island, sailing between it and another island, Princess Royal. That decision would later line them up with the errant log floating in the middle of the water.

The combination of the more conservative route and the log collision seemed sure to bump them out of first place. But they just wanted to finish the race with the boat—and themselves—in one piece. The racers managed to tilt the boat on its side and pop off the log. They slowly floated until daylight. Somehow, there was no damage. But the encounter rattled some members of the team. *Could they swim to shore? Was sleeping in a life jacket really overkill?*

The following evening, Sail Like a Girl came gliding back into cell service near the city of Prince Rupert. It was a starless night, and the moon was shining over the ocean when Anna got a text message from her son. It read: "Mom, you're in the lead!"

Disbelief reigned. How long had it been since he sent that message? But a race tracker GPS device on board confirmed the text wasn't stale—they were still in first and heading into the home stretch to Alaska. Fans from as far away as Germany followed the team's progress using that same race tracker, cheering them on from a distance.

On the final day, the women wore red-colored gear, appearing as bright pinpricks surrounded by various shades of steely blue—the water,

Team Sail Like a Girl

the mountains, the sky—in race footage. The wind died down in the last several hours to the finish line, pushing the boat's arrival from morning to lunchtime, to maybe by when the bars closed . . . to after midnight. It was a fitting end to a race that involved more than seventy-five hours of biking. Family, friends, and cheering supporters lined the docks in Ketchikan— including a little girl who'd fallen asleep in a cart awaiting their arrival. As they coasted toward shore, the women hugged and popped bottles of champagne.

Sail Like a Girl beat over forty other vessels to become the first all-women's boat to win the Race to Alaska—clocking 750 miles in 6 days, 13 hours, and 17 minutes. "I didn't realize what an impact it would have," Jeanne said. "It continues to blow me away." The victory also marked the first time a monohull boat won the race. All other winning teams prior to 2018 had raced in a boat with multiple hulls, like a catamaran. Aimee sometimes finds all the attention on the team's femininity "bittersweet," given that winning the race on a new type of boat is an accomplishment in its own right, no matter who is doing the sailing. "It shouldn't be that big of a deal," she said.

The win and a subsequent nonprofit (also called Sail Like a Girl) formed by some of the team members have helped advance women's visibility in sailing, where let's just say there's room for improvement. Some team-mates raced again in 2019 or helped prepare race crews in 2020. They've also hosted racing clinics and given over fifty presentations about the race and what it means to get outside your comfort zone. "That's what it's really all about," Aimee said. "It's just taking things that are bigger than you." Maybe that's sleep deprivation and cold, dark waters, or maybe it's something closer to home.

Jeanne wants girls leading the boats, not just getting on them. "I wanted more women to find a way behind the mast," she said, where the leadership positions are. Maybe that little girl asleep at the finish line in Alaska won't just be watching sailing races someday. She'll be competing in them, leading a boat to greatness on the vast blue sea.

KELLY KULICK JUST WANTS TO BOWL

By Lyndsey D'Arcangelo

I don't bowl much, if at all. It's not that I don't enjoy it occasionally; it's just not my sport of choice. I know plenty of people who do bowl, though—friends, relatives, even my tattoo artist. He talks about bowling sometimes when he's inking me up. We discuss a variety of things actually, from politics and philosophy to old-school rap and true crime. Our range of discussion knows no boundaries.

Still, the conversation usually comes back to sports. He often asks for my opinion on trending sports-related topics, which unsurprisingly always circles back to the inequity between men's and women's athletics. While he marvels at the disparity, I forgive his naivety. He expects the world to be straightforward and devoid of bullshit, and that is part of why I have chosen him as my tattoo artist. Also because he tells me bluntly when any of my tattoo ideas are lame.

During one particular conversation about his bowling league, he lamented that it was short of participants.

"I was like, just let women into the league," he said.

This glaringly obvious solution made sense to most of the guys in his league. But one was flat-out against it and—big surprise—couldn't give a reasonable explanation why. Regardless, the majority ruled. Women were allowed to play. Hooray.

"And guess what?" My tattoo artist grinned. "The best bowler in the league is not only a woman—she's playing on this dude's team."

We shared a laugh at the irony, and I wondered if he'd ever heard of Kelly Kulick.

Kelly is one of the most accomplished women bowlers in the world. Among her many accolades, she's the first woman to win a major national title against men. That's right. In 2010, Kelly competed head-to-head against male bowlers in the Professional Bowlers Association (PBA) Tournament of Champions in Las Vegas. She picked them off one by one, like pins at the end of the bowling lane, on her way to a historic victory.

> ## She picked them off one by one, like pins at the end of the bowling lane, on her way to a historic victory.

"I always wanted to be a professional bowler since I was in the fifth grade. And I envisioned myself winning a national title against men," Kelly told me during a phone conversation. "I honestly believed I could do it and I thought I was going to do it sometime in the future. It's almost like I had visualized it at such a young age that I made it happen."

Tennis legend and women's sports advocate Billie Jean King knows a thing or two about competing against men, having won the infamous Battle of the Sexes match over Bobby Riggs in 1973. Of Kelly's victory, she said that it's "not only historic, [but] it serves as a motivational and inspirational event for girls and women competing at all levels all around the world."

The thing is, Kelly didn't set out to make history. She just wanted to bowl. Like any athlete, she simply wanted to be the best in her sport.

Kelly's professional career began after she graduated from Morehead State University, where she was a three-time National Collegiate Bowling Coaches Association (NCBCA) Most Valuable Player, two-time Collegiate Bowler of the Year, and two-time Women's All-American. In 2001, Kelly joined the Professional Women's Bowling Association (PWBA) and took home the trophy for Rookie of the Year. Her first PWBA title came shortly after, when she won the 2003 US Women's Open.

But then Kelly's bright future dimmed as quickly as the lights in an old blue-collar-town bowling alley: The PWBA folded in the middle of the year.

The PWBA originally formed in 1960, but like many women's sports leagues and organizations, it struggled to gain a foothold; endured years of financial instability; and lacked proper sponsorship, marketing, and overall support. The organization underwent a variety of changes over the years, losing members to rival associations and merging with others. It reemerged in 1998 with new financial backing and a fresh logo—only to fold four and a half years later when sponsors became sparse.

Without the PWBA or a competitive tour to make money and continue bowling, some women retired. The end of a professional women's bowling league was also the end of their careers. Others joined leagues outside of the United States. But not Kelly.

Miraculously, the previously men's-only PBA decided to open its doors to women in April 2004. On June 4, 2006, Kelly became the first woman to earn a PBA Tour exemption, which allowed her to compete in every PBA event of the 2007 season.

Competing against men never intimidated Kelly. Like the many fearless women athletes before her who believed in themselves and their talent, and bucked the system along the way while giving a metaphorical finger to the falsehoods and stereotypical beliefs about women in sports, Kelly embraced the challenge. If reaching her goal of being the best bowler she could be meant going up against men in the process, well, by all means, *bring it on*.

"Even when the PWBA folded, I was still trying to keep my dream alive. I was staying active and competitive. So it was nice to have a job again," Kelly said. "In qualifying for the men's tour, it's miraculous what I achieved."

After the dissolution of the PWBA, both the PBA and the United States Bowling Congress (USBC) eventually went on to sponsor numerous women's events, plenty of which Kelly competed in—and won. Over the course of her career, Kelly won six major women's bowling titles and forty medals in team and individual international competitions. Still, she says the PBA tournament title she won against men was the most satisfying of all.

It's easy to understand why.

Like Kelly, I was a tomboy growing up. I wasn't a bowler, but I played a lot of soccer and football. For a long time, up until high school, I played against boys. I was the only girl in neighborhood empty-lot tackle football games and on youth soccer teams, and it didn't faze me one bit. I saw myself as one of the guys, but more in the sense of talent and skill. Even back then, I was keenly aware of the sentiment that girls were less than boys when it came to athletic ability. It had been hammered into my head via social settings, overheard derogatory commentary at sporting events, my coaches' demeanor, and even my parents. More than anything, I wanted to prove them all wrong, even if my young tomboy brain didn't realize exactly why. Like Kelly, I knew that I was more than good enough to compete against the boys; I was better than most.

Needless to say, I won my fair share of games, scored goals, made touchdowns, and tackled some boys to the ground so hard they had trouble getting up. Every time—and I mean every single time—I lined up across from a boy on the soccer or football field and managed to wipe the smug grin off his face with one single move or play, it was a glorious, indescribable high. To have been able to accomplish such a feat on a professional level would have been an incredible experience. And it was one that Kelly got to have.

When Kelly sets the scene of her tournament win, she paints a picture of a crowded bowling alley in the center of Las Vegas nightlife with people spilling over one another on the bleachers behind her. The audience was so raucous, it felt more like a college football championship game than a bowling event. Kelly fed off that energy. As the top male bowlers continued to make mistakes, Kelly remained steady and focused on the task at hand. With every strike she threw, the cheers grew louder.

The growing momentum and anticipation followed Kelly into the semifinal match. It was as close as a pair of thoroughbreds galloping toward the finish line at the Kentucky Derby. To make it to the finals, Kelly would have to close out her turn with two strikes, and then knock down at least seven pins in her final throw.

When she got the first strike, the announcer on the televised broadcast proclaimed, "She's the modern-day Annie Oakley!" Then came the second strike. And then a third, which propelled her into the final match with the crowd firmly behind her.

Kelly faced off against the No. 1 seeded player in the tournament, Chris Barnes. Unlike that bro in my tattoo artist's bowling league, Barnes knew better than to underestimate his opponent based on her gender. When asked in the prematch interview about competing against a woman for the championship, Barnes replied, "Gender doesn't have anything to do with it. She's proven it all [tournament] long."

In the final, Barnes appeared unsure of himself and indecisive in his throws. Kelly, on the other hand, was on a mission. Even when Barnes made a run of strikes and put on the pressure, she never wavered. Kelly tossed four strikes in a row without batting an eyelash, effectively ending Barnes's comeback. She won the title 265–195 (300 is a perfect game), blowing the minds of the male spectators and the roof off the bowling alley simultaneously.

As Kelly lifted the trophy high above her head, she pointed to the crowd and yelled, "Girl power!" Then she handed it to her mom.

Kelly's success wasn't just an individual win. It was a win for girls everywhere who grew up believing they could play sports as well as or better than the boys. I imagine there's no feeling in the world that compares to winning a championship trophy or tournament title as a professional athlete. But to do so as the underdog—as a woman in a "man's field"—must taste even sweeter.

For women in sports, men's accomplishments and records have always been the benchmark. Men are the measuring stick. Instead of being evaluated on the basis of their own talent and merit on the playing field, women are judged on how they stack up against men. So naturally, despite many victories against women in her career, the attention bestowed upon Kelly following her 2010 PBA tournament win was unlike anything she'd experienced previously. She signed with clothing lines, appeared in commercials, and became the first bowler in now-defunct *ESPN The Magazine*'s annual body issue in 2011, which featured nude athletes from across different sports.

"Bowling is often pushed under the rug, and I don't always think we get the credit we deserve as athletes," Kelly said. "It's an any-size-fits-all sport. You can be any size, any shape, any gender, any skill level. It accepts all. So when I was offered the opportunity [to be in the body issue], I jumped at it. And I felt comfortable enough in my skin to do it."

As is often the case, the attention on Kelly began to wane as the years rolled by, and as more and more women continued to achieve incredible heights and recognition in a variety of sports. Eventually, after a twelve-year hiatus, the PWBA reemerged from the ashes in 2015 with the backing of the USBC. Its new slogan is "Bowl Fearless." With the recent rise of women's sports and increase in viewership, coverage, participation, and financial backing overall, hopefully this iteration of the PWBA will keep growing in the right direction.

These days, Kelly is still bowling. But at forty-seven years old, she's nearing the end of her professional career. She's accomplished everything she set out to do in the bowling lane and then some—including being a featured character in a *Spider-Man* comic book. In 2019, she was inducted into the USBC Hall of Fame. Since 2021, she's continued to pass on her knowledge and experience as the head coach of the coed Junior Team USA.

"I love bowling. It knows no gender. Everything is the same—the lane, the weight of the bowling ball, the pins," said Kelly. "But I want to find something else to do too. I've lived out of a suitcase since I was twelve."

Can't say that I blame her. When you dedicate your entire life to a certain craft and reach all your goals in the process, there comes a point where you start asking yourself: What now?

Maybe someday, in retirement, Kelly will join a local coed bowling league, where I'm sure she'll shock the shit out of the guys who want to keep their boys' club sacrosanct. Which reminds me. Next time I go in for a tattoo, I need to tell my guy about Kelly. It's important to pass along the triumphs of amazing women athletes, because it's a crucial part of history that is often overlooked, undercelebrated, and more often than not, unrecognized. Only by sharing these specific stories do we change that overall narrative.

Maybe my tattoo artist will pass on Kelly's story to that guy in his league. Maybe he'll be surprised that a woman can be the best. Or maybe by now he's finally figured that out. In the end, his opinion doesn't matter much. Women don't need men's approval or acceptance in sports or anywhere else. They keep kicking ass regardless.

"WE'RE FREAKIN' BADASS WOMEN."

Alex Morgan

They Find Power in Teamwork

A NEW PATH FORWARD FOR INCARCERATED WOMEN

By Camber Scott-Clemence

Some big names are attached to the Los Angeles–based Angel City Football Club. Natalie Portman, America Ferrera, Julie Uhrman, Jennifer Garner, Serena Williams, Mia Hamm, and Billie Jean King are all part owners of this National Women's Soccer League team.

But some of the most important names are those most folks will never know—those who have never walked a red carpet or won an Olympic medal or received adulation from seventeen million Instagram followers. They are the names of those who benefit from some of the most critical work ACFC does: what happens off the pitch.

Since its inception in 2020, ACFC has been focused on creating something different—not just a pro sports team, but something by the community, for the community.

"We are very intentional with our values—we aren't all over the place or reactive. We are consistent, and ultimately, when it comes to community impact, we care about the organization we're serving and less about what the national public perception might be," explained Tiffany Rubin, director of community impact at Angel City FC. "We're up-front with what we're doing. We're up-front with how we're doing it. So if you're buying into ACFC, you're also buying into our values."

And there may be no place where ACFC's values shine through more clearly than in their partnership with the Twinning Project.

The Twinning Project is a UK-based nonprofit that aims to reduce recidivism rates through the power of sport. Since its 2018 launch, more than seventy professional soccer teams in England and Wales have partnered with prisons to bring soccer to inmates. The Twinning Project's stated goals are "to improve [inmates'] mental and physical health, and well-being, and obtain a qualification which will help improve their life chances and gain employment on release."

The Twinning Project teaches social and personal responsibility through sport, using soccer to help prisoners develop teamwork, leadership, and conflict-management skills. Furthermore, it aims to give inmates training so that, upon release, they can get jobs as soccer coaches or refs.

Mostly, it is men's prisons and men's soccer clubs involved in the Twinning Project. But ACFC is changing that: They're a professional women's team partnering with a women's prison, the Century Regional Detention Facility in Lynwood, California.

"Jails and prisons were never really designed to house women, and our systems weren't prepared to deal with the complexities of women being primary caretakers and what it means when you take a woman out of society," explained Dr. Melissa Kelly, acting director of gender responsiveness in the Los Angeles Sheriff's Department. "The LA County Board of Supervisors created my unit to ensure that we are looking at and understanding the trajectories of incarcerated women, trying to make the system more responsive to their situation, bringing some equality into how they're treated, what their resources are, and trying to impact their journey—whether they stay with us or go back into the community. It's like the saying 'A rising tide lifts all boats,' and that's the mentality my department tries to take."

In that rising tide, two volunteer coaches—Danielle Hanson and Fish—are the pilot boats, guiding and assisting others. Dani and Fish, ACFC x Twinning Project program specialists, work together to create the curriculum for this program and coach the women.

When Dani and Fish began working with the first cohort of twelve inmates in 2023, they focused on what it means to be a coach and a leader. With Abby Wambach's *Wolfpack* as their class textbook, Dani and Fish

Fish and Dani Hanson

helped the women discover their influence and how to use it to drive change within themselves, their families, and their communities.

"One of the biggest moments for me was from our first cohort," Fish told me. "We were about four weeks in, and one of the women found out that she was sentenced to life and—as you can imagine, or try to imagine—showing up to play soccer when you're processing that news isn't the first thing you want to do. But she did. There is so much resilience in her and how she cared for the team. She was a leader, and she really cared. She started to share some of her story, some of the context around her charge, and as she spoke, all I could see was the human, and I felt so much compassion for her and standing up for her family, and by no means did I see a monster. Who knows what any of us would have done in her position."

Fish understands the humanity in the women they coach. "There's nothing different between me and them at the end of the day, except sports. Sports got me back on track because I was also heading down a bad path," they said. "But I played soccer, and my family had money for it, and I had all the opportunities, responsibilities, support, and privilege that comes with that. Other than that—we're the same. We have all lost people, we've all loved people, and at the end of the day, we would do anything to protect our families."

While Dani and Fish are technically there to educate the women in the cohort, they both agree that talking with and learning more about the inmates is an invaluable education for them as well. Their time as coaches has shifted their perspective, softening them and allowing them to provide people with more grace and understanding.

It shifts the perspectives of the women playing too. You can see it when they change into their Twinning Project kits for the first time.

When serving time, your sense of self can slip away. Every prisoner dresses in blues—just another woman in a sea of ill-fitting uniforms, being called by a last name or number. However, the women in the ACFC x Twinning Project cohorts are granted a reprieve from their everyday mandated dress while practicing. Though the soccer kits are also technically uniforms, they symbolize something greater: teamwork, collaboration, learning, camaraderie. Every person I spoke to for this story brought up the moment the women changed into their kits for the first time. They light up, and the atmosphere immediately transforms.

As one woman put it: "When I took off my blues and put on the jersey, it felt relaxing, and my mind was focused on something else besides jail. It's more than just going outside and kicking the ball; it's about teamwork and the willingness to change."

With that, the women transform from inmates to teammates, ready for six weeks of learning, having fun, playing soccer, and talking—sometimes

> "It's more than just going outside and kicking the ball; it's about team-work and the willingness to change."

about the game and sometimes about much more difficult topics.

The goal is always to ensure that the women feel safe enough to share with their teammates and coaches. One particular moment stands out to Dani and Fish. They spoke with the women about what their practices of self-reflection looked like. One woman who didn't regularly speak up began to share—how she didn't love herself, how negative her internal voice was. For her, it was a moment of growth and trust. She gave her teammates the opportunity to support her. And they did, immediately.

Of course, the women also learn about the actual game. In the beginning, they start with the simple stuff—passing with a partner, the techniques and dynamics of moving with the ball—before moving into games of 3v3.

"They're playing in smaller than a half-court area—it's tight," said Dani, who played in high school and also coaches youth soccer. "We have twelve women in there who've never played soccer before, and it can be madness in such a small space. But they do so well and are really into it—you can see their joy, [the] willingness to learn and to mess up."

Coming into the program, there are lots of opportunities to "mess up," as Dani puts it. The women create a culture that empowers them to cheer each other on regardless of the situation or circumstance. Through the course of the six-week program, the women cover support, communication, awareness, teamwork, adaption, and reflection.

"*Wolfpack* was such a perfect choice for the curriculum," said Fish. "When I hear *wolfpack*, it kind of harkens to this idea of a chosen family. There's this idea that your wolfpack is just your family or your kids or your partner—but we can also choose our wolfpack, and the cohort becomes that. But there's also a conscious switch of like—oh, this is what a wolfpack should feel like. For some of these women, our cohort is the first healthy example of support they've experienced."

Dr. Melissa Kelly is focused on the short-term impacts right now. Her team looks at how the women interact with others in the facility and with their families and whether they see an improvement in self-confidence. She wants to answer questions like: Have they learned anything? Do they feel better about themselves? Are they engaging in positive behavior? After playing soccer, are they enrolling in other exercise classes?

"I know that women who go in there have done better for themselves," said Dr. Kelly. "And I think that's important not to gloss over—sometimes it's about those little wins."

Everyone involved in the program, from the staff at the Los Angeles Sheriff's Department to the program's sponsors at Pasadena City College to the women of the cohort, believe that the redemptive potential of sport and human connection can address immediate challenges and fundamentally reshape trajectories.

"Being in the Twinning Project cohort has reminded me that being incarcerated is temporary," said one participant. "I can put this behind me. Being on the team was a blessing, and I have learned to grow with positivity and build my self-esteem."

Of course, the program is not a silver bullet that solves the problems of recidivism or incarceration rates.

"It's complicated," Dr. Kelly acknowledged. "But just because it's difficult doesn't mean we walk away from the problem—we still need a solution. I know it sounds cliché, but if we can positively impact one woman's life, who knows how many other lives we're touching? Eighty percent of our women are mothers; these programs matter because they impact her life, the life of her family, and the lives of so many generations down the line."

The reality is that the ACFC x Twinning Project program is about far more than just women playing soccer. After all, sports aren't merely about learning new physical skills. The real progress for athletes—the part that sticks with them long after the game is over—is about discovering newfound confidence, expanding social skills, and embracing challenges with resilience.

Whether on or off the pitch, at any stage and in any situation, the power of sports persists, shaping individuals into stronger and more empowered versions of themselves.

As one woman said at the completion of her time with the ACFC x Twinning Project program: "Thank you for teaching me what you know about life and a sport that has so much to offer, and mostly thank you for teaching me that being a woman, I have rights to have anything this world has to offer. You guys came and not only taught us but also learned with us. I want to thank my wolfpack for bringing the hustle and showing up even when we were having bad days. You guys softened a part of me that I didn't know I still had. Thank you for allowing me to shine in the midst of darkness."

AFTERWORD

Legacy is a complicated, layered thing.

When you pick up a basketball for the first time, you probably aren't thinking about becoming a professional. You aren't imagining world records, or championships, or magazine covers, or published books. The only thing that matters in that moment, really, is the relationship between you and the ball. The first act of building a legacy happens right there, with that initial belief in yourself.

You learn to dribble. To shoot. Maybe most importantly—as I learned—to pass. You may enter your sport by yourself, but there's a whole world within that's anything but solo. You now stand in the footprints of everyone who has played before you. That's when act two of legacy begins. Understanding who and what came before you and how you create what comes next. It's the choices you make as a teammate. The training. The barriers you come up against . . . and break down. The fans. The expectations you set and the ones you defy. Yes, the wins, but also the heartbreaks. Every single part of it defines your legacy.

And then comes act three. When it's all said and done. Legacy isn't just about wins and losses and rings, but about what you do for those coming behind you. The paths you create. The reaching back and pulling up. Knowing that being a champion is also about championing others.

True legacy is generational.

This book is about understanding legacy in all its acts. Our stories are ever interconnected. Here's to the past, the now, and the next.

—Sue Bird

THE CONTRIBUTORS

Shireen Ahmed is an award-winning multiplatform sports journalist and instructor of sports journalism and sport media at Toronto Metropolitan University. She is a global expert on Muslim women in sports and internationally recognized for her work on racism and misogyny in sports. She lives in Toronto, Canada.

Maitreyi Anantharaman is a staff writer at *Defector*, where she covers women's basketball. She lives in Detroit.

Erica Block is a sports journalist and former collegiate lumberjack sports competitor who lives in New York. She covers Yankees baseball and the Brooklyn Nets for the YES Network, and she was previously the lead researcher for Jomboy Media and an editor for MLB.com. Follow her on X at @ericadaleblock and on Instagram at @edblock.

Allison Torres Burtka is a freelance writer and editor in metro Detroit. Her writing about women athletes has appeared in the *Guardian*, *Outside*, *Runner's World*, *Women's Running*, espnW, *Sierra*, and other publications. She received the 2023 Asian American Journalists Association's Excellence in Sports Reporting Award. You can see more of her writing at atburtka .journoportfolio.com, and you can follow her on Instagram and Threads at @allisonburtka.

Mollie Cahillane is the media reporter at *Sports Business Journal* and was previously the senior TV reporter at *Adweek*. A Northwestern University graduate, she's passionate about all things (women's) sports. Cahillane lives in Brooklyn. Follow her on X at @MollieCahillane and on Instagram at @mollkc.

Frankie de la Cretaz is a Boston-based independent journalist whose work focuses on the intersection of sports, gender, and culture. They are the coauthor of *Hail Mary: The Rise and Fall of the National Women's Football*

League, and their writing has appeared in the *New York Times*, *Sports Illustrated*, and more. You can find them on social media platforms at @thefrankiedlc.

Lyndsey D'Arcangelo is an award-winning writer, author, and women's sports advocate based near Buffalo, New York. Her work has appeared in Awful Announcing, *The Athletic, Just Women's Sports*, NBC, *The Ringer*, ESPN/espnW, *Fast Company*, and more. She is the coauthor of the critically acclaimed women's sports history book *Hail Mary: The Rise and Fall of the National Women's Football League*.

Lauren DeLaunay Miller is an award-winning author and journalist from California. Her reporting focuses on health, the environment, and immigration. She is the author of *Valley of Giants: Stories from Women at the Heart of Yosemite Climbing.*

Saeedeh Fathi is the first female editor of a sports magazine in Iran and has been a sports journalist for over twenty years. In 2024, she won the International Sports Press Association's Defending Freedom of Press Award. She was arrested and held in Evin Prison in 2022 during the Woman, Life, Freedom movement because of her work. She is now based in Vienna, Austria.

Kylie Mohr is an award-winning freelance journalist based in Montana. Her stories appear in *National Geographic*, *The Atlantic*, NBC News, *Vox*, *High Country News*, and more. Find her at @thatsMohrlikeit and kyliemohr.com.

Chidinma Iwu is a writer interested in deep dives and analyses into underreported phenomena that underpin large subcultures. She writes about technology, sustainability, gender justice, and culture as we know it for *Worth*, *Paste*, *Fast Company,* Shondaland, *Daily Dot*, *ARTnews*, and more. She is based in Abia, Nigeria. Find her articles at chidinmaiwu.com or follow her on X at @Chidxnma.

Deepti Patwardhan is a freelance sportswriter based in Mumbai, India, with almost twenty years of experience. She writes mainly on Olympic sports and has penned articles for the BBC, *Mint Lounge*, and fiftytwo.in.

Lauren J. S. Porter is a Brooklyn-based storyteller and strategist with a specialty in sports and entertainment. Her nearly decade-long career has included branded and editorial work that has garnered her industry-wide recognition, including her feature on the 2023 Forbes 30 Under 30 list in Sports. To see a catalog of Lauren's work, visit laurenjsporter.com or follow her across social media at @thelaurenline.

Tonya Russell is a New Jersey–based freelance journalist specializing in health and wellness. She's written for the *New York Times*, the *Washington Post*, *Runner's World*, and more. When she's not running, she's probably marathon training or hiking with her dogs.

Leila Sales is the author of eight critically acclaimed novels for children and young adults. After more than a decade as an acquiring editor at Penguin Random House, she's now director of publishing for TOGETHXR, where she works to amplify women's stories. She lives in Austin, Texas. Visit her at leilasales.com or follow her at @LeilaSalesBooks.

Safaa Sallal is a Syrian journalist based in Damascus. She has been working in the media for ten years and specializes in solutions journalism, society, and humanitarian reporting. She has also covered the war in Syria. She produces and presents a program titled "A' Fikra" (I Have an Idea) for Lana TV, an online Syrian TV channel.

Camber Scott-Clemence is a journalist with a focus on women's sports, queer life, and social change. As a devoted mother and partner living in Florida, Camber creates writing grounded in authenticity, drawing inspiration from her own life experiences.

Aileen Weintraub is a women's health and lifestyle journalist whose work has been featured in the *Washington Post*, *Oprah Daily*, the BBC, and many others. Her book *Knocked Down: A High-Risk Memoir* is a University of Nebraska Press bestseller, and her middle-grade social justice book, *We Got Game: 35 Female Athletes Who Changed the World*, was honored as a Mighty Girl Best Book of the Year. She is based in New York.

SOURCES

They Are Trailblazers: Katie Hnida and the Women of College Football

One fall evening . . . Lyndsey D'Arcangelo, *Hail Mary: The Rise and Fall of the National Women's Football League* (New York City: Bold Type Books, 2021).

Hnida's time at Colorado . . . Katie Hnida, *Still Kicking: My Dramatic Journey as the First Woman to Play Division One College Football* (New York City: Scribner, 2006), book summary.

Not only was she . . . Rick Reilly, "Another Victim at Colorado," *Sports Illustrated*, January 20, 2005.

It's obvious Katie . . . Jemele Hill, "Hnida finds peace in telling story," *ESPN The Magazine*, December 8, 2006.

They Build the Community They Need: Indigenous Women Run

And so, in 2018 . . . Verna Volker, interview by Allison Torres Burtka, December 27, 2023.

Now, the Instagram . . . Native Women Running Instagram page, accessed June 3, 2024, https://www.instagram.com/native_women_running/.

So far, they've . . . Volker interview.

A Navajo coming-of-age . . . Ariel Shirley, "Running at Dawn: A Diné Cultural and Health Teaching," The University of Arizona Health Sciences, April 22, 2019.

For many native . . . Volker interview.

The statistics for . . . Denise V. D'Angelo, "Rape and Sexual Coercion Related Pregnancy in the United States," *American Journal of Preventive Medicine*, November 5, 2023.

Each year on . . . The White House, "A Proclamation on Missing Or Murdered Indigenous Persons Awareness Day, 2022," May 4, 2022.

When they run . . . Rosalie Fish, interview by Allison Torres Burtka, December 26, 2023.

Rising Hearts' Running . . . Jordan Marie Whetstone, interview by Allison Torres Burtka, January 19, 2024.

Many children were . . . Zach Levitt et al., "War Against the Children," *The New York Times*, August 20, 2023.

When Rosalie committed . . . Fish interview.

Rosalie is a Brooks . . . Fish interview.

In 1980, she . . . Allison Torres Burtka, "Patti Catalano Dillon," *Starting Line 1928*, December 21, 2023.

A Native Women . . . Volker interview.

Before the opening . . . TCS New York City Marathon Instagram, November 5, 2023, https://www.instagram.com/nycmarathon/.

They Never Stop Swimming: Two Friends Take Lessons from the Water to the World

Madeline Murphy Rabb and Ann E. Smith, interview by Lauren Porter, December 27, 2023.

In 1964 . . . "Remembering A Civil Rights Swim-In: 'It Was A Milestone,'" *NPR*, June 13, 2014.

To this day, African American children . . . Jeff Wiltse, "Racial History of American Swimming Pools," *NPR*, May 6, 2008.

They Find Strength in One Another: The Atlanta Dream Enter Politics—and Won

We all know . . . Elizabeth Williams, "How the WNBA helped flip Georgia blue," *Vox*, January 11, 2021.

A prospective buyer . . . Tony Rehagen, "The Best Team You've Never Seen," *Atlanta Magazine*, September 1, 2012.

attachment to Atlantans . . . Angel McCoughtry, "Feeling Good Again," *The Players' Tribune*, February 8, 2018.

attachment to Loeffler . . . Jerry Brewer, "Kelly Loeffler chose pandering over principle, and WNBA players won't forget," *The Washington Post*, July 10, 2020.

its own name . . . Richard Fausset, "How Kelly Loeffler Went From Atlanta Elite to Trump Loyalist," *The New York Times*, October 21, 2020.

Here's what folks . . . Greg Bluestein, "Kelly Loeffler will say she's 'pro-military, pro-wall, and pro-Trump' at Senate intro," *The Atlanta Journal-Constitution*, December 4, 2020.

McCoughtry would wonder . . . Bria Felicien, "Former Dream star Angel McCoughtry speaks about Loeffler, WNBA season," *The Atlanta Journal-Constitution*, July 8, 2020.

against gun violence . . . Ava Wallace, "'Why am I different?' Behind this WNBA player's activism was a search for an answer," *The Washington Post*, June 22, 2019.

politicizing women's bodies . . . Lindsay Gibbs, "WN-BA's star players speak out against anti-abortion bills," *ThinkProgress*, May 24, 2019.

Taylor's mother, Tamika . . . Ta-Nehisi Coates, "The Life Breonna Taylor Lived, in the Words of Her Mother," *Vanity Fair*, August 24, 2020.

out her window . . . Renee Montgomery, "The WNBA Star Turned Team Owner Who Found Her Voice," *The Daily Beast*, September 25, 2022.

This is what . . . Renee Montgomery, "When the W Comes Back, I Won't Be There," *The Players' Tribune*, June 19, 2020.

approached the league . . . Gina Mizell, "Why Does the W.N.B.A. #SayHerName? Ask Angel McCoughtry," *The New York Times*, September 2, 2020.

a voice for . . . Gillian R. Brassil, "'We Will Be a Voice for the Voiceless': The W.N.B.A. Season Is Dedicated to Breonna Taylor," *The New York Times*, September 20, 2020.

I adamantly oppose . . . Greg Bluestein and Bria Felicien, "Loeffler opposes WNBA's plan to spread 'Black Lives Matter' message," *The Atlanta Journal-Constitution*, July 7, 2020.

Montgomery reached out . . . Renee Montgomery (@ReneeMontgomery), "Dear @SenatorLoeffler …. I'm pretty sad to see that my team ownership is not supportive of the movement & all that it stands for. I was already sitting out this season & this is an example of why. I would love to have a conversation with you about the matter if you're down?" Twitter, July 7, 2020.

I can't believe I . . . Layshia Clarendon (@Layshiac), "I can't believe I ever stepped foot in Kelly's house and shared a meal with her. It's actually really hurtful to see her true colors. I had no idea while I played for ATL she felt this way. Happy to own us as long as we stay quiet and perform," Twitter, July 7, 2020.

Before she entered . . . Candace Buckner, "How Kelly Loeffler's politics made her a WNBA villain," *The Washington Post*, August 29, 2020.

The 144 met . . . Sean Gregory, "'We Did That': Inside the WNBA's Strategy to Support Raphael Warnock—and Help Democrats Win the Senate," *Time*, January 7, 2021.

Sue Bird suggested . . . Percy Allen, "Led by Sue Bird, WNBA players wear shirts in support of Dream co-owner Kelly Loeffler's Senate opponent," *The Seattle Times,* August 5, 2020.

Within two days . . . Angele Delevoye, "The WNBA influenced the Georgia Senate race, new research finds," *The Washington Post*, November 30, 2020.

It's always been . . . Williams, "How the WNBA helped."

McCoughtry had similar . . . Cassandra Negley, "'We're all one country, we're all Americans': Aces star Angel McCoughtry views jersey initiative as seed for change," *Yahoo! Sports*, July 3, 2020.

Williams lay awake . . . Williams, "How the WNBA helped."

Winning never felt . . . Layshia Clarendon (@Layshiac), "Winning never felt so damn good," Twitter, January 6, 2021.

The WNBA Board . . . Atlanta Dream, "WNBA Approves Sale of Atlanta Dream to Larry Gottesdiener," *WNBA*, February 26, 2021.

She Keeps Climbing: Farahnaz Ibrahimi Finds a Home in Sports

Farahnaz Ibrahimi, interview by Lauren DeLaunay Miller, January 4, 2024.

They Fight Discrimination: Baring It All for Title IX

The bill declares that . . . Steve Wulf, "Title IX: 37 words that changed everything," *ESPN*, March 22, 2012.

While sports are not mentioned . . . Tom Goldman, "Title IX revolutionized female athletics but advocates say it's been a constant fight," *NPR*, June 23, 2022.

NCAA itself is not liable . . . Steve Berkowitz, "U.S. senator wants answers from NCAA's Mark Emmert on efforts to promote Title IX compliance," *USA Today*, June 17, 2022.

We used the leftover men's boats . . . Roseanna Means, interview by Madeleine Kline, "Interviews of the Margaret MacVicar Memorial AMITA Oral History Project," Massachusetts Institute of Technology, Institute Archives and Special Collections, June 2, 2017.

After practices at the Robert Cooke Boathouse . . . Rehan Melwani, "Behind the Venue: A history of Gilder Boathouse and the protest behind its concept," *Yale* Daily News, April 12, 2021.

This culminated in an event . . . Wulf, "Title IX: 37 words that changed everything."

These are the bodies Yale is exploiting . . . Steve Wulf, "Title waves," *ESPN*, May 29, 2012.

No effective action has been taken . . . Wulf, "Title waves."

The story ran the following day . . . David Zweig, "Yale Women Strip To Protest a Lack Of Crew's Showers," *The New York Times*, May 4, 1976.

a group of more than a dozen . . . Rebekah Riess, "Current and former college athletes sue NCAA, alleging Title IX violations over transgender policy," *CNN*, March 15, 2024.

the equal protection clause in the US Constitution does not . . . The Equal Protection Clause, ConstitutionCenter.org/the-constitution/amendments/amendment-xiv.

This legislation is just a way . . . David Wharton, "As Title IX turns 50, it plays a surprise role in transgender athlete access debate," *Los Angeles Times*, June 20, 2022.

the current push to weaponize Title IX . . . Frankie de la Cretaz, "New State of the Game," *YES!*, February 27, 2023.

thirty-two female University of Oregon athletes . . . Rebecca Cohen, "32 female University of Oregon athletes file Title IX lawsuit against the school," *NBC News*, December 1, 2023.

former students from James Campbell High School . . . David W. Chen, "Sex Discrimination Case in Hawaii Could Change High School Sports Across the U.S.," *The New York Times*, October 22, 2022.

That kind of stuff is still happening . . . Wulf, "Title waves."

They Are Mothers: Athletes Demand More Maternity Rights

almost died while giving . . . Serena Williams, "How Serena Williams Saved Her Own Life," *ELLE*, April 5, 2022.

Olympians had to fight . . . Dave Sheinin, "Nursing Olympians no longer have to choose between the Tokyo Games and their babies," *The Washington Post*, June 30, 2021.

Allyson Felix had to publicly . . . Allyson Felix, "My Own Nike Pregnancy Story," *The New York Times*, May 22, 2019.

Icelandic professional soccer player . . . Sara Björk Gunnarsdóttir, "What Happened When I Got Pregnant," *The Players' Tribune*, January 17, 2023.

Getting pregnant is the kiss . . . Alysia Montaño and Lindsay Crouse, "Nike Told Me to Dream Crazy, Until I Wanted a Baby," *The New York Times*, May 12, 2019.

finding that it's safe . . . Kari Bø, Raul Artal, Ruben Barakat, Wendy Brown, Gregory A. L. Davies, Michael Dooley, Kelly R. Evenson, Lene A. H. Haakstad, Karin Henriksson-Larsen, Bengt Kayser, Tarja I. Kinnunen, Michelle F. Mottola, Ingrid Nygaard, Mireille van Poppel, Britt Stuge, Karim M. Khan, "Exercise and pregnancy in recreational and elite athletes: 2016 evidence summary from the IOC expert group meeting," Olympics.com, 2016.

went public in the New York Times . . . Montaño and Crouse, "Nike Told Me to Dream."

went public in the New York Times . . . Felix, "My Own Nike Pregnancy Story."

Nike amended their contract . . . Cassandra Negley, "Nike eliminates wage reductions while pregnant after taking heat from runners like Allyson Felix," *Yahoo! Sports*, August 16, 2019.

Other brands like Athleta . . . "Athlete, Mother, Activist," press release, Athleta, 2019.

Other brands like . . . *Burton* . . . "How We're Supporting Women and Families on The Burton Team," *The Burton Blog*, May 16, 2019.

Other brands like . . . *Brooks* . . . Jen A. Miller, "Maternity Leave for Sponsored Runners," *The New York Times*, May 18, 2019.

For us, we've been . . . Monique Lamoureux-Morando and Jocelyne Lamoureux-Davidson, "The Lamoureux twins on motherhood, career: Why can't we 'have it all'?" *MSNBC*, May 29, 2019.

The Women's Tennis Association (WTA) changed . . . Courtney Nguyen, "WTA Tennis," wtatennis.com, 2018.

Training camp included five . . . "USWNT roster selected for training camp ahead of April friendlies against Ireland," *SoccerWire*, March 28, 2023.

guaranteed athletes fully paid maternity leave . . . "Collective Bargaining Agreement 2020," *WNBPA*, 2020.

Dearica Hamby filed a discrimination lawsuit . . . Myron Medcalf, "Dearica Hamby files discrimination lawsuit against Aces," *ESPN*, October 4, 2023.

Skylar Diggins-Smith claimed . . . Alexa Philippou, "Skylar Diggins-Smith says she can't use Mercury facilities," *ESPN*, August 3, 2023.

had to hide her first pregnancy . . . Alexis Jones, "I Hid My Pregnancy For 14 Weeks While Playing Pro Basketball." *Women's Health*, February 10, 2020.

Icelandic soccer player Sara Björk Gunnarsdóttir . . . Gunnarsdóttir, "What Happened."

This is not 'just business . . .' Gunnarsdóttir, "What Happened."

Change is not linear . . . Amira Rose Davis, "Athlete Moms Are Fighting Battles in and out of Sports. What Will It Take to Win?" *Global Sport Matters*, July 19, 2023.

Because of the ongoing coronavirus pandemic . . . Sheinin, "Nursing Olympians."

Former Olympian Kara Goucher . . . Montaño and Crouse, "Nike Told Me to Dream."

Canadian basketball player Kim Gaucher said . . . Henry Bushnell, "Olympic organizers reverse course, will allow breastfeeding athletes to bring babies to Tokyo," *Yahoo! Sports*, June 30, 2021.

They wouldn't be allowed . . . Johnny Diaz, "The Spanish swimmer Ona Carbonell says she is disappointed to leave her breastfeeding son at home," *The New York Times*, August 8, 2021.

Employers are required to provide . . . "Family and Medical Leave Act," U.S. Department of Labor, Wage and Hour Division.

the United States ranks last . . . Mary Beth Ferrante, "UNICEF Study Confirms: The U.S. Ranks Last For Family-Friendly Policies," *Forbes*, June 21, 2019.

Right now, we don't treat pregnancy . . . Frankie de la Cretaz, "Women Athletes Are Disrupting Traditional Perspectives on Parenthood," *Global Sport Matters*, September 21, 2021.

She Speaks Her Truth: Daria Kasatkina and the Politics of Sexuality

This notion of . . . Daria Kasatkina, interview by Vitya Kravchenko, "Cancellation of Russian Sports," YouTube, 2018.

Dasha was born . . . "Kasatkina Darya Sergeevna - RNI 14136," Russian Tennis Tour, July 2014.

her parents, Tatyana . . . Alexey Filippov, "Who is Daria Kasatkina, the Rising Star of Russian Tennis?" *Russia Beyond*, September 19, 2018.

Excelling as a . . . "Daria Kasatkina," profile, WTA, 2024.

I was in . . . Tom Kershaw, "Daria Kasatkina: I want to be able to respect myself when I look in the mirror," *The Times*, July 1, 2023.

It's just like . . . Kershaw, "Daria Kasatkina."

Dasha's parents weren't . . . Kershaw, "Daria Kasatkina."

It's difficult when . . . Kershaw, "Daria Kasatkina."

In 2021, Dasha . . . "Russians prevail over Swiss to win fifth Billie Jean King Cup championship," *WTA Tennis*, November 6, 2021.

In 2022, Dasha . . . "Daria Kasatkina," WTA.

In response to . . . AFP, "Wimbledon Bans Russian and Belarusian Players, but ATP Slams 'Unfair' Move," *The Moscow Times*, April 20, 2022.

I want to ask . . . Michael Steinberger, "How the War in Ukraine Turned Tennis Into a Battlefield," *The New York Times*, August 29, 2023.

Since returning to . . . RFE/RL's Russian Service, "A Supreme Court Case Strikes Fear In Russia's LGBT Community," *Radio Free Europe, Radio Liberty*, November 27, 2023.

In Russia, Dasha . . . RFE/RL, "A Supreme Court Case."

Living in the . . . Kasatkina, interview by Kravchenko, "Cancellation of Russian Sports."

I couldn't hide . . . Kershaw, "Daria Kasatkina."

Dasha's family is . . . Kershaw, "Daria Kasatkina."

It's hard not . . . Kershaw, "Daria Kasatkina."

All these parts . . . David Kane, "Daria Kasatkina reclaims the narrative with popular YouTube channel at Roland Garros," Tennis.com, June 2, 2023.

They Fight the Patriarchy: The Reggae Girlz

derisory prize money . . . Noé Amsallem, "Women's World Cup: Despite rising prize money, female players still paid four times less than men," *Le Monde*, August 11, 2023.

Vietnam and beyond . . . Jeré Longman, "Worlds Apart: Cup's Expansion Brings the Games of a Lifetime," *The New York Times*, July 16, 2023.

defunded their women's . . . Tom Hamilton, "Jamaica's struggle for equality and respect at World Cup," *ESPN*, August 2, 2023.

led online fundraisers . . . Timothy Rapp, "Bob Marley's Daughter Cedella's Fundraising Helped Fund Jamaican Women's Soccer," *Bleacher Report*, June 4, 2019.

qualified for the . . . Jayanta Oinam, "Why Jamaican women are Caribbean Football Union's flag-bearers," *FIFA*, 2022.

They launched another . . . Matias Geez, "Bob Marley instilled a love of soccer in his daughter, Cedella. Now she's changing the lives of women and girls in Jamaica," *CNN*, August 2, 2023.

long, pain-filled statement . . . Cora Hall, "Bunny Shaw, Tennessee soccer players call out Jamaican Federation over Women's World Cup preparation," *Knoxville News Sentinel*, June 15, 2023.

every goal attempt . . . Kimberly Richards, "Jamaica's Reggae Girlz Make History At 2023 Women's World Cup," *HuffPost UK*, August 3, 2023.

round of sixteen . . . Darreonna Davis, "Jamaica Becomes First Caribbean Nation To Reach Round 16 In Women's World Cup," *Forbes*, August 2, 2023.

They Trust Their Bodies: Smashing a Taboo in Women's Sports

Pallant-Browne could have ignored . . . Emma-Pallant Browne (@em_pallant), Instagram, May 24, 2023.

Shame and criticism . . . "Periods in Sports: Impact of Menstruation on Female Athletes," *Tribes for Good*, August 14, 2022.

A 2021 study of elite . . . Phoebe Read, Ritan Mehta, Craig Rosenbloom, Elena Jobson, and Katrine Okholm Kryger, "Elite female football players' perception of their menstrual cycle stages on their football performance," National Library of Medicine, December 29, 2021.

The US women's soccer team . . . Katie Kindlan, "How tracking their periods helped USA women's soccer team win the World Cup," *Good Morning America*, August 8, 2019.

According to research funded . . . Kaitlin Baslasaygun, "Nike's approach to solving the biggest problem for girls in sports," *CNBC*, June 18, 2023.

Of the fourteen thousand athletes surveyed . . . "Product Innovation and Resources to Help Those Who Menstruate Stay in Play," Adidas, June 2021.

Unfortunately, studies show . . . Hanna Laske, Mara Konjer, and Henk Erik Meier, "Menstruation and training," *International Journal of Sports Science and Coaching*, December 8, 2022.

In a 2023 POPSUGAR article . . . Kristine Thomason, "Why There's Still Stigma Around Periods in Sports, According to Athletes and Coaches," *POPSUGAR*, November 4, 2023.

Unsurprisingly, period stigma . . . Christine Yu, "Silencing Period Talk Hurts Athletes," *Time*, May 16, 2023.

As late as the 1970s . . . Aimee Crawford, "Exclusion to Exclusivity: The History of Women Running the New York City Marathon," *Sports Illustrated*, November 5, 2021.

Holmes said during . . . Anna MacSwan, "Protesters at Wimbledon urge end to all-white dress code due to period concerns," *The Guardian*, July 9, 2022.

British tennis pro Heather Watson . . . "Heather Watson Breaks Period Taboo at Australian Open," *CBC Radio*, January 27, 2015.

The Orlando Pride is . . . Jaclyn Diaz, "Soccer's Orlando Pride ditches players' white shorts over period concerns," *NPR*, March 1, 2023.

The Irish women's rugby team . . . Kieran Pender, "'Monumental change': football tackles the impact of periods on performance," *The Guardian*, July 1, 2023.

Fu Yuanhui, went viral . . . "Fu Yuanhui Talks About Her Period," YouTube, August 16, 2016.

The result was a social media firestorm . . . Emily Feng, "Uninhibited Chinese Swimmer, Discussing Her Period, Shatters Another Barrier," *The New York Times*, August 16, 2016.

having her period . . . Mai Yoshikawa, "Retired Olympian reshaping conversation around athletes' periods," *Kyodo News*, November 11, 2020.

an organization established . . . Swaroop Swaminathan, "The battle before competition: India's women athletes talk about periods and how they fight the pain," *The New Indian Express*, July 20, 2021.

Famed golfer Tiger Woods . . . Associated Press, "Tiger Woods goes viral for all the wrong reasons after tampon 'prank,'" *NBC News*, February 17, 2023.

Woods later apologized . . . Emily Tannenbaum, "The Tiger Woods Tampon 'Prank' Isn't Just Offensive—It's Stupid," *Glamour*, February 18, 2023.

Fifty elite athletes . . . "Hannah helping push period conversation in sport," *Aquatics GB*, March 8, 2023.

She Believes: Failure Is Not an Option for Jenny Hoffman

Jenny Hoffman, interview by Tonya Russell, January 2, 2024.

They Row Together: Recovery on Water

But, fortunately for . . . Tara Hoffmann, interview by Allison Torres Burtka, December 21, 2023.

It turns out . . . Sue Ann Glaser, interview by Allison Torres Burtka, December 22, 2023.

Even just being . . . Michail Georgiou, "A population-based retrospective study of the modifying effect of urban blue space on the impact of socioeconomic deprivation on mental health, 2009–2018," *Nature*, July 19, 2022.

ROW is part . . . "Participating Programs," Survivor Rowing Network website.

ROW members range . . . Hoffmann interview.

The many side effects . . . Linda A. Koehler, David W. Hunter, Anne H. Blaes, and Tufia C. Haddad, "Function, Shoulder Motion, Pain, and Lymphedema in Breast Cancer With and Without Axillary Web Syndrome: An 18-Month Follow-Up," *Physical Therapy*, June 2018.

The prevailing wisdom . . . Justin C. Brown and Kathryn H. Schmitz, "Weight Lifting and Physical Function Among Survivors of Breast Cancer: A Post Hoc Analysis of a Randomized Controlled Trial," *Journal of Clinical Oncology*, July 2015.

And studies have . . . Jamie DePolo, "Exercise Before and After Breast Cancer Diagnosis Improves Survival, Reduces Recurrence Risk," Breastcancer.org, June 4, 2020.

And studies have . . . Rikki A. Cannioto et al., "Physical Activity Before, During, and After Chemotherapy for High-Risk Breast Cancer: Relationships With Survival," *Journal of the National Cancer Institute*, June 4, 2020.

Tara later started . . . Hoffmann interview.

Ninety-five percent . . . "Why Rowing for Breast Cancer?" Recovery on Water website.

ROW has grown . . . Hoffmann interview.

They Decide What to Wear: Breaking Through Dress Codes in Sports

In some countries like Iran . . . Shireen Ahmed, "Iranian women's fight for liberty is cut from similar cloth to women's battle for justice in sports," *CBC Sports*, September 27, 2022.

In Saudi Arabia . . . The Athletic Staff, "Special report: Saudi Arabia, women's football's next frontier?" *The Athletic*, October 12, 2023.

I have said it many times . . . Shireen Ahmed, "Forcing women out of clothing is just as violent as forcing them into it," *TRT World*, July 2021.

An entire global campaign started . . . "Pink offers to pay bikini bottoms fine for Norway women's handball team," *BBC*, July 26, 2021.

The team was tired . . . Claire Galofaro, "German Olympic gymnastics team, tired of 'sexualization,' wears unitards," *The Associated Press*, July 25, 2021.

They Resist: Iranian Women Athletes and Soccer Fans Rewrite the Rules of Engagement

My friends were all against it . . . Nasim, interview by Saeedeh Fathabadi, January 2, 2024.

I never thought I'd feel so safe . . . Maryam, interview by Saeedeh Fathabadi, January 2, 2024.

In the early years . . . Zahra Ghanbari, interview by Saeedeh Fathabadi, January 3, 2024.

That day, on the rooftop . . . Parisa Pourtaherian, interview by Saeedeh Fathabadi, January 3, 2024.

She Cheers for Herself First: Justine Lindsay, NFL Cheerleader

It was the best . . . Brooke Cersosimo, "First openly transgender NFL cheerleader Justine Lindsay a 'face of the possible,'" NFL.com, November 19, 2022.

Black women are still . . . Paige Skinner, "Black Cheerleaders Are Calling for Change. Will the NFL Listen?" *Allure*, October 11, 2020.

Which is why she wanted . . . Rose Minutaglio, "Loud and Proud," *ELLE*, September 18, 2023.

More than three hundred anti-LGBTQ+ bills . . . "Anti-LGBTQ Bills in 2022," Human Rights Campaign, 2022.

In 2022, thirty-two trans people . . . "An Epidemic of Violence: Fatal Violence Against Transgender and Gender Non-Conforming People in the United States in 2022," Human Rights Campaign, 2022.

two transgender women . . . Hollie Silverman and Harmeet Kaur, "2 transgender women killed in shootings at separate Charlotte hotels," *CNN*, April 16, 2021.

Everything that I'm going through . . . Minutaglio, "Loud and Proud."

I just felt like when . . . Paige Skinner, "Justine Lindsay Is The NFL's First Openly Trans Cheerleader," *BuzzFeed News*, June 4, 2022.

pro cheerleading has come with . . . Laura Vikmanis and Amy Sohn, "Little to Cheer About," *The New York Times*, April 14, 2018.

In 2019, professional dancers . . . "Rams make NFL history with male cheerleaders at Super Bowl LIII," NFL.com, 2020.

Seeing people that looked like me . . . Minutaglio, "Loud and Proud."

I was around people who . . . Minutaglio, "Loud and Proud."

The Panthers fan base ranked . . . Neil Paine, Harry Enten, and Andrea Jones-Rooy, "How Every NFL Team's Fans Lean Politically," *FiveThirtyEight*, September 29, 2017.

the North Carolina legislature . . . Li Zhou, "North Carolina is the latest in a wave of states passing anti-trans laws," *Vox*, August 17, 2023.

We are in the South . . . Minutaglio, "Loud and Proud."

Bans on trans athletes . . . Jules Gill-Peterson, "Transgender Compromise," *Sad Brown Girl*, May 3, 2023.

My goal is to create . . . Skinner, "Justine Lindsay."

She had a shaved head . . . Minutaglio, "Loud and Proud."

Being out on the field . . . Cersosimo, "First openly transgender NFL cheerleader."

She Opens Doors: Rani Rampal, Queen of the Field

Rani Rampal, interview by Deepti Patwardhan, January 3, 2024.

She Builds a Legacy: Maybelle Blair Came Out to Play Ball

Maybelle Blair, interview by Mollie Cahillane, December 27, 2023.

They Were the Few: Finding the Freedom to Just Play

Baylor Henry, interview by Lauren Porter, December 18, 2023.

Hailey and Myla Barnett, interview by Lauren Porter, December 19, 2023.

She Builds a Space for Women: Timber Tina and Lumberjack Sports

You would literally . . . Tina Scheer, interview by Erica Block, December 28, 2023.

Log rolling contests . . . Lew Freedman, *Timber! The Story of the Lumberjack Championships*, (Madison, WI: The University of Wisconsin Press, 2011), 102.

as early as the 1930s . . . Associated Press, "Cloquet Girl Takes Championship," *The Escanaba Daily Press*, August 15, 1937.

Scheer plans to build . . . Leticia Baldwin, "Logroller hoping to branch out," *The Bangor Daily News*, February 17, 1996.

When a Wisconsin woman . . . Leticia Baldwin, "A Tradition That's Aged In Wood," *The Bangor Daily News*, August 22, 1997.

It was very . . . Dave Smith, interview by Erica Block, February 5, 2024.

In 2004, tragedy . . . "Tina Scheer: Logging Sports Entertainer," Mentor of the Week, UMission.org, July 28, 2013.

They Keep Competing: When Age Is Just a Number

the average ages . . . Nick Zaccardi, "Olympic women's gymnastics median age in 20s for first time in decades," *NBC Sports*, July 14, 2021.

99 percent of the athletes . . . Aldo F. Longo, Carlos R. Sifredi, Marcelo L. Cardey, Gustavo D. Aquilino, and Néstor A. Lentini, "Age of peak performance in Olympic sports: A comparative research among disciplines," *Journal of Human Sport & Exercise*, Vol. 11 No. 1, 2016.

I can't answer . . . Scott Bregman and Katerina Kuznetsova, "Oksana Chusovitina: 'If I set some goal... I have to achieve it.'" Olympics.com, March 31, 2022.

an ordinary person . . . Jo Gunston, "The Legend of Oksana Chusovitina: why does gymnastics mean so much to the eight-time Olympian?" Olympics.com, March 16, 2022.

When I retire . . . Scott Bregman, "Oksana Chusovitina: 'Why should I leave the sport if it brings me joy?'" Olympics.com, June 20, 2023.

I continue training . . . Amanda Turner, "Ageless Chusovitina Turns 33," *International Gymnast*, June 19, 2008.

It doesn't matter . . . Nancy Armour, "44-year-old gymnast has to wait to see if she qualified for Tokyo Olympics," *USA Today*, October 4, 2019.

As long as long as I'm able . . . Bregman, "Oksana Chusovitina: 'Why should I leave?'"

she trained constantly . . . Lizzie Feidelson, "What If Everything We Know About Gymnastics Is Wrong?" *The New York Times*, August 1, 2021.

it's keeping those . . . Dave Tilley, "Chellsie Memmel Discusses Her Elite Gymnastics Comeback!" *SHIFT Movement Science*, August 10, 2020.

Training now is . . . Scott McDonald, "'Wired Differently,' 2000 Olympic Diving Champ Laura Wilkinson Returns At Age 39," *Team USA*, March 6, 2017.

If Nolan Ryan . . . Andrew Abrahams, "Olympic Swimmer Dara Torres on Her 30-Year Journey with Asthma: 'It's the Challenges That Motivate Me,'" *People*, February 2, 2024.

You have to listen . . . Andy Frye, "Dara Torres Still Stays Crazy Busy After A 12-Medal Olympic Career," *Forbes*, August 12, 2019.

I thought I would never . . . Frye, "Dara Torres Still Stays Crazy Busy."

I am at . . . John Crumlish, "At 48, eight-time Olympian Oksana Chusovitina is still soaring through her second youth," *International Gymnast*, October 12, 2023.

I think it's good . . . "IG Online Interview: Oksana Chusovitina (Uzbekistan)," *International Gymnast*, February 2001.

We're all equal . . . Bregman and Kuznetsova, "Oksana Chusovitina: 'If I set some goal.'"

I have never felt . . . Bregman and Kuznetsova, "Oksana Chusovitina: 'If I set some goal.'"

she worked as . . . Lois Elfman, "Deanna Stellato has found fulfillment off the ice," *IceNetwork.com*, February 4, 2010.

If I could talk to . . . OlympicTalk, "Deanna Stellato-Dudek becomes oldest woman to win world figure skating title in pairs' victory," *NBC Sports*, March 21, 2024.

I hope a . . . Lawrence Yee, "Canadian Ice Skater Becomes Oldest Female World Figure Skating Champion at Age 40," *People*, March 21, 2024.

331 senior appearances . . . Neil Davidson, "Canadian soccer great Christine Sinclair announces retirement from international play," *CBC*, October 20, 2023.

potentially the fittest . . . Derek Van Diest, "VAN DIEST: Humble superstar Christine Sinclair puts team ahead of individual goals," *Toronto Sun*, June 8, 2019.

a decade older . . . Katherine Ellen Foley and Dan Kopf, "Women soccer players are younger than men because they can't afford longer careers," *Quartz*, June 18, 2019.

At the 2023 . . . Davidson, "Canadian soccer great Christine Sinclair."

I guess there's . . . Kristina Rutherford, "Canadian hockey legend and four-time Olympic gold medalist Hayley Wickenheiser on her incomparable career, her retirement, and what she'll miss most about the game she loves." The Interview with Kristina Rutherford, *Sportsnet*, 2017.

It's impossible to . . . Scott Bregman, "Oksana Chusovitina comes out of retirement to target 2022 Asian Games," Olympics.com, September 30, 2021.

We are women . . . Bregman, "Oksana Chusovitina: 'Why should I leave?'"

She Says Watch Me Do It: Alia Issa Takes On the World

In my first international tournament . . . Alia Issa, interview by Safaa Sallal, January 6, 2024.

At the beginning of her training . . . Dionisis Koubaris, interview by Safaa Sallal, January 6, 2024.

I have never been ashamed of my daughter . . . Fatima Al-Naggar, interview by Safaa Sallal, January 8, 2024.

They Aren't Intimidated: The Mayan Rebels

I was the only . . . Mark Viales, "Las Amazonas de Yaxunah, women warriors of Mexican softball," *Mexico News Daily*, August 28, 2023.

Growing up in Yaxcabá . . . Adam Williams, "An Indigenous Women's Softball Team Beats Opponents, and Machismo," *The New York Times*, November 17, 2021.

We have seen . . . Mark Viales, "Maya battle cry: barefoot softball players swing at Yucatán's macho taboos," *The Guardian*, October 30, 2023.

[Aradillas's] story really touched me . . . Julio Guzmán, "Fighting Machismo And Inequality: Mayan Women's Softball Team Pitches Against Discrimination," *Birmingham Times*, November 23, 2021.

a group of Denver . . . Carlos Rosado van der Gracht, "Broncos cheerleaders play a friendly softball game against the Amazonas of Yucatán," *Yucatán Magazine*, May 31, 2022.

Manuel Rodriguez, a . . . Jennifer Bubel, "Manny Rodriguez receives special jersey," *Diario AS*, October 14, 2022.

Roughly a year . . . Magali Alvarez, "Historic! Yaxunah Amazons get their first win in the U.S." *The Yucatan Times*, September 13, 2023.

The sports-retail business . . . Nicole Ducouer, "Champion What Moves You: Calling on Diverse Creators as Face of the Campaign," *Business Wire*, September 13, 2023.

I used to really. . . Williams, "An Indigenous Women's Softball Team."

The way a number . . . Mark Viales, "Women Maya softballers brush off machismo insults to become Mexican superstars," *NPR*, October 11, 2023.

They Defy Expectations: Sail Like a Girl

Jeanne Goussev, interview by Kylie Mohr, December 21, 2023.

Aimee Fulwell, interview by Kylie Mohr, January 2, 2024.

Anna Stevens, interview by Kylie Mohr, January 5, 2024.

The race's website . . . "Race to Alaska Explained," Race to Alaska (R2AK) website.

Meet the women . . . Alexa Philippou, "Sail like a girl: How an all-female team made history and won the 750-mile Race to Alaska," *The Seattle Times*, July 16, 2018.

The water here . . . "R2AK 2018 Clip of the Day - DAY THREE," Northwest Maritime, YouTube, June 20, 2018.

The sailboat continued . . . "R2AK 2018 - WOULD I GO?" Northwest Maritime, YouTube, September 8, 2017.

On the final . . . "R2AK 2018 Clip of the Day - DAY SEVEN," Northwest Maritime, YouTube, June 24, 2018.

Family, friends, and . . . "R2AK 2018 Clip of the Day - DAY SEVEN," YouTube.

As they coasted . . . "R2AK 2018 Clip of the Day - DAY SEVEN," YouTube.

She Beats Everyone: Kelly Kulick Just Wants to Bowl

Kelly Kulick, interview by Lyndsey D'Arcangelo, Fall 2023.

Tennis legend and . . . Bob Sansever, "Meet Kelly Kulick: The Billie Jean King of Bowling," *Twin Cities Pioneer Press*, August 18, 2015.

"Kelly Kulick," United States Bowling Congress website.

"Bodies We Want 2011: Kelly Kulick," *ESPN*, 2011.

Lucas Wiseman, "Column: Olympics Reject Bowling Again And The Reason Is Obvious," FloBowling, February 21, 2019.

Professional Women's Bowling Association homepage.

They Find Power in Teamwork: A New Path Forward for Incarcerated Women

We are very . . . Tiffany Rubin, interview by Camber Scott-Clemence, January 2024.

The Twinning Project is a UK-based . . . Hilton Freund, interview by Camber Scott-Clemence, January 2024.

Since its 2018 . . . Freund interview.

The Twinning Project's stated goals . . . Freund interview.

The Twinning Project teaches . . . Freund, interview.

Jails and prisons . . . Dr. Melissa Kelly, interview by Camber Scott-Clemence, March 2024.

One of the . . . Fish, interview by Camber Scott-Clemence, March 2024.

While Dani and . . . Fish and Danielle Hanson, interview by Camber Scott-Clemence, March 2024.

When serving time . . . Fish and Hanson interview.

As one woman put it . . . Unnamed program participant, provided by ACFC, March 2024.

The goal is always . . . Fish and Hanson interview.

They're playing in . . . Fish and Hanson interview.

Coming into the . . . Fish and Hanson interview.

Wolfpack was such . . . Fish and Hanson interview.

Dr. Melissa Kelly is focused . . . Kelly interview.

I know that women who . . . Kelly interview.

Being in the Twinning . . . Unnamed program participant, ACFC.

It's complicated, Dr. . . . Kelly interview.

As one woman said at . . . Unnamed program participant, ACFC.

Quotation Pages

All you can . . . Sue Bird, "Sue Bird 'always wanted' to become part of Storm's ownership group," *ESPN*, April 29, 2024.

Being strong is . . . Serena Williams, "Serena Williams: The Power of Unapologetic Greatness," *Allure*, January 10, 2019.

I just need . . . Chloe Kim, "Snowboarder Chloe Kim on Hot Cheetos, Roxy, and Going for Gold (Again) at the 2022 Winter Olympics," *Elle*, November 9, 2020.

The only thing . . . Simone Biles, "What's changed for Simone Biles since Tokyo Olympics? Her magic is 'limiting social media,'" *Today*, July 17, 2024.

When I think . . . Simone Manuel, "Swimmer Simone Manuel on Why Being Strong Doesn't Mean Being Superhuman," Tonal.com, February 17, 2022.

Whenever people say . . . Alex Morgan, "How Soccer Star Alex Morgan Is Handling Team U.S.A.'s 'Crushing' Quarterfinals Loss," *People*, August 17, 2016.

I am lucky . . . Serena Williams, "Serena Williams: I'm Going Back to Indian Wells," *Time*, February 4, 2015.

If you can . . . Sue Bird, "Take Action," *The Players' Tribune*, June 6, 2018.

If you just . . . Chloe Kim, "Olympic gold medalist Chloe Kim shares her No. 1 tip for success," *CNBC*, February 14, 2018.

People believe in . . . Caitlin Clark, Clevelanddotcom Instagram, April 7, 2024, http://www.instagram.com/clevelanddotcom.

We're freakin' badass . . . Alex Morgan, "Alex Morgan UNCUT: "We're Freakin' Badass Women! (espnW SportsCenter)," YouTube, October 31, 2017.

PHOTOGRAPHY CREDITS